Drunks & Other Poems of Recovery
a collection of poetry

☙

by Jack McCarthy

Write Bloody Publishing
America's Independent Press

Austin, TX

WRITEBLOODY.COM

Copyright © Jack McCarthy 2012

No part of this book may be used or performed without written consent from the author, if living, except for critical articles or reviews.

McCarthy, Jack.
1st edition.
ISBN: 978-1938912-14-6

Interior Layout by Lea C. Deschenes
Cover Designed by Anthony Wyborny
Proofread by Melinda Aguilar
Edited by Derrick Brown
Type set in Bergamo from www.theleagueofmoveabletype.com

Write Bloody Publishing
Austin, TX
Support Independent Presses
writebloody.com

To contact the author, send an email to writebloody@gmail.com

DRUNKS & OTHER POEMS OF RECOVERY

Drunks & Other Poems of Recovery

Drunks 13

The Story 18

That Promise 20

Uncle Fred, or So That's What Happened to Jaxon Hardy 21

Office 26

My Lunch with George 28

Errand 33

For Joe Williams, 1918-1999 36

Christmas Story 43

Cornerback 48

Arthur M. 52

Waiting for a Dudley 57

Frank & Dewey 60

The Samaritan 63

Hatcheck 66

Kenmore Square 69

To the Beautiful Young Mother Who
Misunderstood Me at the AA Meeting 71

Snapshot at an AA Meeting 74

Epithalamion: A Few Words for Kathleen 75

Neponset Circle 79

Substances 82

For Ruth Read, on Her Seventy-Fifth Birthday 86

Ruth Read Approaching 80 89

Ruth Read's Last Ninth Step 96

The Divorced Catholics of Jaffrey, New Hampshire 102

The Sacrament 106

Drunks: the Story of the Poem 108

Author's Afterword 111

Drunks

We died of pneumonia in furnished rooms
where they found us three days later
when somebody complained about the smell
we died against bridge abutments
and nobody knew if it was suicide
and we probably didn't know ourselves
except in the sense that it was
always suicide
we died in hospitals
our stomachs huge, distended
and there was nothing they could do
we died in cells
never knowing whether we were guilty or not

We went to priests
they gave us pledges
they told us to pray
they told us to go and sin no more, but go
we tried and we died

We died of overdoses
we died in bed (but usually not the Big Bed)
we died in straitjackets
in the DTs seeing God knows what
creeping skittering slithering
shuffling things

And you know what the worst thing was?
The worst thing was that
nobody ever believed how hard we tried

We went to doctors and they gave us stuff to take
that would make us sick when we drank
on the principle of so crazy, it just might work, I guess
or maybe they just sent us places like Dropkick Murphy's
and when we got out we were hooked on paraldehyde
or maybe we lied to the doctors

and they told us don't drink so much
just drink like me
and we tried
and we died

We drowned in our own vomit
or choked on it
our broken jaws wired shut
we died playing Russian roulette
and everybody thought we'd lost
we died under the hoofs of horses
under the wheels of vehicles
under the knives and boot-heels of our brother drunks
we died in shame

And you know what was even worse?
was that we couldn't believe it ourselves
that we had tried
and we died believing that
we didn't know what it *meant* to try

When we were desperate or hopeful
or deluded or embattled enough to go for help
we went to people with letters after their names
and prayed that they might have read the right books
that had the right words in them
never suspecting the terrifying truth
that the right words, as simple as they were
had not been written yet

We died falling off girders on high buildings
because of course ironworkers drink
of *course* they do
we died with a shotgun in our mouth
or jumping off a bridge
and everybody knew it *was* suicide
we died under the Southeast Expressway
with our hands tied behind us
and a bullet in the back of our head
because *this* time the people that we disappointed

were the *wrong* people
we died in convulsions, or of "insult to the brain"
incontinent, and in disgrace, abandoned
if we were women, we died degraded
because women have so much more to live up to
we tried and we died and nobody cried

And the very worst thing
was that for every one of us that died
there were another hundred of us, or another thousand
who wished that we *would* die
who went to sleep praying we would not have to wake up
because what we were enduring was intolerable
and we knew in our hearts
it wasn't ever gonna change

One day in a hospital room in New York City
one of us had what the books call
"a transforming spiritual experience"
and he said to himself

I've got it
(no you haven't, you've only got part of it)

and I have to share it
(now you've ALMOST got it)

And he kept trying to give it away
but we couldn't hear it
the transmission line wasn't open yet
we tried to hear it
we tried and we died

We died of one last cigarette
the comfort of its glowing in the dark
we passed out and the bed caught fire
they said we suffocated before our body burned

they said we never felt a thing
that was the *best* way maybe that we died
except sometimes we took our family with us

And the man in New York was so sure he had it
he tried to love us into sobriety
but that didn't work either, love confuses drunks
still he tried and still we died
one after another we got his hopes up
and we broke his heart
because that's what we do

And the very worst thing of all was that every time
we thought we knew what the worst thing was
something happened that was even worse

Until a day came in a hotel lobby
and it wasn't in Rome, or Jerusalem, or Mecca
or even Dublin, or South Boston
it was in Akron, Ohio, for Christ's sake

A day came when the man said I have to find a drunk
because I need him as much as he needs me

(NOW
you've got it)

And the transmission line
after all those years
was open
the transmission line was open

And now we don't go to priests and doctors
and people with letters after their names
we come to people who have been there
we come to each other
and we try
and we don't have to die.

Footnotes to "Drunks"

1. The Big Bed

When I was getting sober in Boston in the early 60s, the old-timers talked about the progression of recovery this way: first you get your teeth back, then you get a job, then eventually you get back in the Big Bed: i.e. the good graces of your wife.

2. The DTs

From Wikipedia: "Delirium tremens (Latin for 'shaking frenzy'), also referred to 'the horrors', 'The Irish Jig' or 'the shakes.') is an acute episode of delirium that is usually caused by withdrawal from alcohol, first described in 1813."

3. Dropkick Murphy's

A lot of people must wonder about this reference. Following is the most authoritative explanation I've been able to find. It's from the website of the rock group, the Dropkick Murphys, in answer to a question about the group's name.

> "John 'Dropkick' Murphy was a football player, a wrestler, and a boxer. He opened up his home as a primitive sort of detox clinic later on in life, and it became the stuff of local legend. You see, his methods were pretty nasty, such as literally tying a 'patient' to their bed and injecting them with horse tranquilizers to help them through the delirium tremens. You'd find anybody from skid row bums to politicians in that joint, so it definitely had a bit of magic about it. The name just seemed to fit."

The "primitive" clinic was just outside of Boston. People told stories about it at meetings. I never heard about horse tranquilizers, but my understanding was that the patients would line up once or twice a day for shots of paraldehyde, a mixture of alcohol and ether. I remember at least one guy who said that when he got out, he was addicted to paraldehyde.

I once rode along when someone was being dropped off there. It was about noon on a Sunday, and our car became the center of attention for a number of men in bathrobes, begging us for a drink.

The Story

Heard once at an AA meeting, never forgotten:

"We're like an island of shipwreck survivors.
Every night we gather around the fire
and tell our stories.

"And the more we tell our stories,
the clearer it becomes:
it isn't many stories we're telling,
it's The Story.

"Sure, the details change
from one telling to another;
but from the beginning,
everyone around the fire
knows where The Story goes,
where The Story always goes.

"And every once in a while
as we sit around the fire, listening,
a cry goes up from the beach,
and we rush down to where
another survivor has washed up.

"We pump the water out of him
and roll him over,
and his eyes open, and he sees
all of us looking down at him,

and he says,
'You are not going to believe
the things that have been happening
in my life,' and we say,
'Try us,' and he begins to talk.

"And as he talks,
we look at each other
and we nod, because he knows
The Story."

Footnote to "The Story"

I wish I could claim that this piece was original with me, but it isn't. I know who wrote it, and I have tried to get in touch with him, but I've had no luck, and no permission to compromise his anonymity. After twenty-plus years, I certainly haven't remembered it perfectly, and in setting it down, I might have stuck in a poetic flourish or two, but all the best lines were his.

That Promise

Spring and summer nights
In cars, with other boys
Not yet quite drunk, nor very dangerous
Savaging the night with rock 'n' roll
Loud talk, loud laughter
Yearning so much, so privately
In the throes of a promise that seemed
Just about to be fulfilled
Copiously, but never was
Never was spelled out, even.
Long gone. Never understood.

It is perhaps a trick of time or age
That makes that yearning
In the memory
Seem by its intensity alone
To be, itself, fulfillment, of a kind.

Uncle Fred, or
So That's What Happened to Jaxon Hardy

In '59 I dropped out of school
and hitched to California to be cool.
I left New York with twenty-three bucks
and arrived in LA hungry, broke,
and almost out of Luckies.

There were pawn shops on Main Street,
and I went up the left side and down the right
trying to hock my overcoat
to get enough to live on for a day.
I thought I was thinking on my feet,
living off the land, travelling light.
The pawnbrokers however all agreed
an overcoat was one thing everyone in LA
didn't need.

I picked up a fellow traveler, older guy,
friendly, good company, not much better off than I,
but with an air of no regrets.
And he had cigarettes.

When we came to the end of the pawnshops, he said,
"I've got a friend on a boat in San Pee-dro—"
(that's the way he said it: Pee-dro)
"professional photographer? He's one of those,

and he's always hunting for people to pose.
You're a fine looking young guy (remember,
I said '59), maybe you'd qualify. I tell you this,
he likes your face, he'll give you steady work,
good pay, and he might have space
till you can get your own place."

I suppose I was pretty naïve,
but it wasn't all that hard to believe;
this was, after all, LA, the myth of discovery.
I just hadn't planned to work my very first day.

My companion didn't want me deciding too casually.
He went on to point out, "You know, models work unusually
long, hard hours. They have to change clothes a lot,
take showers." I assured him that would not
be a problem.

He persisted, "He does the occasional commercial shot,
hotels and stuff. He'd provide the clothes,
but you might have to pose in Bermuda shorts and stuff,
like beside the swimming pool?
You sure that wouldn't bother you?"

I laughed. "I can do Bermudas too."
Then I asked, real casual, "How's he feel
about drinking?" "He likes to have a little fun,
party with the models when the work is done."
I thought what's not to like about this deal?

He went on, "He makes adult films too
before I forget it. He might want you
to pose nude, like with women?"
and I began to get it.

What I thought next is not reflective
on me of any great credit,
but let me put it in perspective.
What was being proposed
was somebody hiring beautiful women
to—who knows? take off all their clothes
and perform with Jax photogenic acts
illegal in many a state.
Whereas I, on my own, in point of fact,
couldn't find girls even willing to date.

Well awright.

My companion led the way to a pay-
phone to call his buddy to come to LA
and pick us up and take us to San Pee-dro.

Meantime, I started thinking about pornography,
not the making but the selling,
and how there's no way of telling
who collects it, people you'd think
wouldn't be caught dead.
I asked myself, "Who's the most unlikely person?"
I answered, "My Uncle Fred."

My Uncle Fred was the straightest,
squarest man I'd ever met.
I'd spent last Christmas night chez Fred.
When we'd arrived he had put a bottle
of beer in everybody's hand
and even though it was an off-brand,
Blatz, I think, I said to myself,
"I guess I'm officially an adult now,
and therefore entitled to drink."

[Now there are those who say
it's possible to drink all day
as long as you keep it to one drink an hour.
I just never knew what it is you're supposed to do
with your hands for the other fifty-two
minutes.]

Naturally I finished my beer ahead
of everyone else and waited with saint-like patience
through endless boring adult conversations
for Uncle Fred to notice the dead
soldiers. I waited till long after
everyone else had finished their beer,
(and they didn't exactly pound them down).
Surely somebody would put in a bid
for a little more Christmas cheer;
but when no one did I took it upon myself
to inquire, jocular, about the next round.

Uncle Fred glared at me
with an expression like
"You think I don't know the score
with you?" Then he actually said,
"There were six bottles in the six-pack
and there are six of us."

Well, God rest ye fucking merry to you too.

Walking with my talent scout
toward a phone booth on Main
Street in LA two months later,
I thought about Uncle Fred:
what makes a man like that
get up in the morning?
I could think of only one answer:
a secret addiction to porn.

I know today that was pretty unfair
but at that time I sincerely believed
that for everything straight in the world, there
had to be a twisted explanation,
and I got this vision of Fred on a caper
locking himself into a room somewhere
opening plain brown paper
leafing with fascination
the pages of his latest treat
having himself a private party—
then stopping, stunned, thinking,

"So that's what happened to Jaxon Hardy."
And that's when I got cold feet.

I felt for years thereafter
it was because of Uncle Fred
that I hadn't achieved hardcore legend,
as the Irish Shaft or something worse.
Sometimes I'd thank him, sometimes curse,
depending how much I was getting on my own.

I carried this story around with me
like a little vignette, an oddity,
never really noticing the shape of the thing,
like a puzzle with one humungous piece missing
out of the middle.

Then one night in an eastern state
at an AA meeting many years later,
I heard a man tell about hitch-hiking to California,
getting picked up by a friendly guy who was willing to ply
him with drinks and stash and a place to crash.
But the speaker ended up chained to a wall,
and he thought that was going to be all
she wrote. He was abused for hours on end
by the friendly guy and his many friends.

He eventually escaped, after days of trying,
but it was clear he thought this had left him
something other than
a man.

But what really caught my attention
was when he mentioned
that the wall he was chained to
was on a boat in San Pee-dro.
That's the way he said it: "San Pee-dro."

And today, when I speak Uncle Fred's name,
it's with a different attitude:
kindness and gratitude;
kindness and gratitude.

Office

The day I turned 21 I waltzed
into the Colonial in Hingham Square.
They asked me for ID and because
I'd let my driver's license lapse—
because I didn't have a car any more—
I showed them my Air Force discharge
(general under honorable conditions,
for reasons I have never understood
but which must have had something to do
with an unpublicized compassion
for patently obvious absolute losers
that sometimes affects even the military).
The actual document mentioned nothing
about the restriction that if I ever
wanted back *into* the service,
I would need a waiver personally signed
by the Secretary of Defense. Suffice to say,
for me, that wasn't a deal-breaker.

I think it was George, the Colonial's owner,
who served me that day, though it may
have been Henny the bartender,
as it often was over the next months,
during which my friends came to
refer to the Colonial as my "office."

One Saturday night we gathered at the bar
and after a couple of beers my friends asked,
"What are we gonna do tonight?"
and I thought, "We're *doing* it,"
but I had already learned to guard my tongue
as soon as I had a few drinks in me,
and I washed those words back down
with a long swallow.

The "friends" I'm talking about
were guys my own age who
did other things during the day
and typically came in only on their way
to someplace else, as distinct from
the regulars at the Colonial
who were my *de facto* friends,
my band of brothers
in the grand adventure
of the drinking life.

Over those six months, I don't think
there were six days that I didn't claim
a place at the bar, usually for hours at a time.
Many of those days I didn't particularly
want to go there, didn't particularly want to
drink, but I was afraid that if I
didn't show up, I'd *miss* something.

Strange now. The only thing I can remember
that ever actually *happened* at the Colonial
was this guy Rusty, who worked for Hingham Lumber,
had a full set of false teeth and once in a while

he'd ask Henny for a glass of water
and take his teeth out and set them in the glass
on the bar, and then he'd talk funny
and we'd all fall about the place laughing.

All those hours, waiting for something to happen.
All those days, afraid I'd miss something.
Half a year of my life, that was
as good as it got, Rusty's teeth.

My Lunch with George

He was the biggest columnist in Boston,
nationally known. Sometimes with the *Globe*,
sometimes the *Herald* (when it was a *good* paper).
Sometimes he'd work in New York for awhile,
but he always came home to Boston.
His column was the first to run in the space
where later ran Patricia Smith, Mike Barnicle.
He'd been entertainment editor of *Life*
in the period when its weekly cover
was seared into national consciousness
at every newsstand, drugstore,
defining for us what was important.
Liner notes by him grace the backs of
several jazz albums that I own.
In those days I didn't believe the rumors
about him and Billie Holiday, but I do now.

He had carte blanche to write about whatever he chose—
often politics, sometimes sports, entertainment.
Sometimes he'd spend a whole column
discussing the distinction between
having "class" and merely having "style,"
or the Spanish "duende,"
who had it and who didn't.
Fred Astaire yes, Gene Kelly no;
Billy Eckstine yes, Vaughn Monroe no.
(Very often it was the black who had it,
white who didn't. He was ahead of his time.)

He was quirky, often arbitrary—
out of nowhere, "Robert Goulet, go to your room."
In the Great Age of White Liberalism,
he was the most liberal of us all.
He did not suffer fools gladly.
And if you were corrupt, he'd trash you
no matter which side you were on.

He admired many writers, Salinger especially.
He frequently referred to the passage in Catcher
where Holden describes liking a book so much
he wants to call the author up and talk about it.
I suspect he felt that was the standard by which
all books should be measured. He loved
Brooks Brothers, the martinis at the Ritz,
and the finnan haddie at Locke-Ober's.

George Frazier went to Harvard from
South Boston and tried to be true to both—
although when busing came along, his loyalty
to South Boston was stretched very thin.
In his Harvard days my mother had
a crush on him that's still a family legend.
He enjoyed a daily constitutional along Carson Beach
and she'd connive to be out there walking the dog
whenever he'd stroll by in his suit and tie.
This must have been early in the many years
she went with my father before they married.
George Frazier never noticed her.
But the dog lived a long and healthy life.
(I remember him; his name was Pal.)

I idolized him. (Not Pal, George Frazier.)
At eleven o'clock on a Thursday night
in November of 1962, after destroying
several billion brain cells over six days
of relentless drunkenness, I looked up Fraziers
in the Boston phone book, and he was listed.
I called him from the room in the Hotel Essex
where I was staying, having been
thrown out of a three-decker in Dorchester.
He answered—I knew he was a night person.

I told him I liked his column so much
I wanted to call him up and talk about it,
and I must not have been slurring too much yet
because he seemed glad of the company.
I asked if he'd like to meet a real-life Holden Caulfield

on an underground weekend in Boston—
that was how the family thought of me
in those days, "a perennial Holden Caulfield"—
and he invited me to lunch at Locke-Ober's on Tuesday.
When I hung up the phone I thought,
"That was one of the nicest people
I ever talked to in my life."

By Tuesday the whole world had changed.
I was three days sober, very sick and shaky.
I felt like an impostor,
that he had made an appointment with
a wild and colorful young guy
and this boring sober person had shown up instead,
somebody doomed to go through life without ever
saying or doing another interesting thing.
Embarrassed, I offered to let him off the hook,
but he was sympathetic, and we sat down.
He ordered a martini and the finnan haddie
and I had tea, clear, with lots of sugar,
and we talked.

We talked about alcoholism,
and he confided casually that he was one too.
He'd tried different cures
but none of them had worked,
it was too hard.

I mentioned that I had started going to AA,
and he said he'd tried,
but couldn't get past the God thing.
He was a divorced Catholic
in the days when those words signified
a life sentence of sad celibacy
punctuated by episodic cycles of sin and repentance,
sin and repentance, till you died—
in the state of repentance if you were lucky.
He was in love with a woman he could never marry.

I shook my head and said I didn't know about that;

the one thing keeping me going
was a saying I had heard at a meeting:
"There's nothing wrong with me today
that a drink won't make a damn site worse."

And George Frazier answered,
"But you know, a drink does make it better.
I know it's only for a little while,
but for that little while,
it *does* make it better."

And in that moment,
from my lofty perch of three days sober,
I took pity on George Frazier,
because I knew something he didn't:
there had to be more to life
than making things better
for a little while.

He invited me to keep in touch,
but I never called him again.
Eventually I stayed sober and finished college,
got married, had kids, and made it all the way back—
I kid you not—to another three-decker in Dorchester.

George Frazier lived ten more years,
died with all those conflicts unresolved.
His death was not sudden,
so maybe he was in a state of repentance,

with probably a cigarette and a martini
on the bedside table.
Maybe the God Thing got worked out face to face.

When George Frazier died Mike Barnicle wrote,
"Tell them they can take the finnan haddie
off the back burner at Locke-Ober's."

In the years that followed,
I became a divorced Catholic,
and just like George Frazier,
I fell in love with another woman.
The difference was that we were able
to get married, in the Church,
surrounded by our children.
Not because we did anything different,
just because things had changed around us.

And sometimes I think about the man
who could have been, if he'd wanted to,
the father of my mother's children.
And I wish I had kept in contact.

And I wish he were here now
because we've been suffering
way too many fools.

Errand

A man is driving home over the Bay Bridge.
He is coming from a treatment program
where he has just said goodbye to alcohol,
but he is not feeling any craving for it.
At this time he has no particular opinion
about the fact of no craving, although later
he will come to recognize it as a unique "gift—"
he will never be comfortable with the word
"miracle," at least as associated
with his own humble concerns.

Not only is the man not feeling any craving,
he is not feeling anything at all.
For years upon years, he has drunk
his feelings away, has battered them
with alcohol to the point where, like all
the people who were once in his life,
his feelings have cut their losses
and cashed in their chips.
The man has been considering suicide
for so long that the idea of going on with life,
of having places to go and things to do—
errands—and feelings about those errands—
will take some getting used to, relearning.

The man is driving in the rightmost lane
because he is in no hurry. He knows
that he is going home, but not why,
except that he is in his car,
and there does not seem to be
any other place to go.

To his right, on the wrong side of the railing
of the bridge, the man sees another man
and understands immediately that the only
possible reason to be there is to jump.

The man's first thought is, "This is the Bay Bridge;
anyone with any class jumps off the Golden Gate.
It's higher, and prettier, songs and poems
have been written about it, and you can look
at a beautiful sunset on the way down.
Why would anyone want to jump off
the Bay Bridge?"

The man, setting aside considerations
of style, stops his car, calls 911, and gets out,
right there on the Bay Bridge, approaches
the jumper, and tries to talk him back.
"It can't be that bad," he says.
"Suicide is a permanent solution
to a temporary problem," he says,
trying to summon up all the analgesic
platitudes that he has half-heard through
the long years of his own half-life.

The jumper is drunk, of course,
and raves that the man has no idea
how bad it is. But he does not jump, not yet,
and the man says, "My friend, you would
never believe how *perfectly* I understand,"
while he edges closer to the jumper,
as though wanting to hear him better.

A Ford pickup pulls around the man's car
and parks, and the driver approaches
quietly. When the driver gets close enough,
he and the man, as if on prearranged signal,
lunge toward the jumper, grab each an arm,
and together pull him back over the railing
and onto the walkway, although he thrashes
furiously.

The man and the driver force the jumper down
onto the concrete. The man sits astride him
and pins him down while the driver goes to
the pickup and gets some rope. He comes back

and they hogtie the jumper and hold him there
until the police arrive—lights flashing,
sirens howling—and take the jumper away.

The pickup driver sticks out his hand to the man,
and the man shakes it briefly, and the driver
gets into his pickup and drives away.
On the rear window of the pickup is a decal
of Calvin pissing on a Chevy emblem.
The man gets back into his car,
but he does not drive away right away.
He does not drive away
because he cannot drive away
because for the first time in many,
many years, the man is crying.

FOR JOE WILLIAMS, 1918–1999

There will be many other nights like this
and I'll be standing here with someone new
there will be other songs to sing
another June, another spring
but there will never be another you.

It was a deep cut
from an album of standards
Joe Williams sang with Count Basie
my favorite song out of
my whole first record collection

that I abandoned
when I had to sell a broken-down Buick
at a place in Warrenton, Virginia
called the Justice Gulf Station
but that's another story.

A lot of those records were bought
so I could learn the words to songs.
When I'd be hitchhiking and I'd find myself
standing by the side of the road
in the middle of nowhere

I would sing at the top of my lungs.
Just recently I've come to see
that at no time in those scuffling years
was I ever happier than in those
roadside serenades to nobody.

Why did I love the Basie version so much?
It's perfect, but that's not sufficient answer,
many records sounded perfect to my ears;
when great musicians get it right,
they get it so right, so often.

And it certainly wasn't that
There Will Never Be Another You
brought back precious, bittersweet memories;
fact was, in my life at that time,
there had never been an initial you.

But for this particular story, all you need
to understand is it had been my favorite,
that I knew it from an album I had lost,
and that, except for one night,
I have never heard it on the radio.

The night I did hear it on the radio
I was hitching back to Boston from Connecticut
where I had fled in the middle of the night
after beating the crap out of an ex-con
old enough to be my grandfather

but that's another story.
Now I'd been sober in AA for a month,
which seemed to be about my limit,
and percolating in the back of my mind
was that great line from Joyce,

"The barometer of his emotional nature
was set for a spell of riot," because
now I had money in my pocket
for the first time in weeks, and from
somewhere out there in the dark

a shot of Seagram's Seven
with my name on it
was sucking that money
toward it like a tractor beam
and I was just along for the ride.

But what was it about Another You?
Maybe the magic lay in the tension

between the sense of loss in the words
and the sweet, swinging, understated,
uncluttered arrangement,

the Count at 3 AM, poring over
the score in some hotel room on the road,
muttering around his cigarette,
"For this one, less is more."
What a concept!

I got picked up by a quiet working guy
who had a long ride home this Friday night.
We listened to radio music
till there it was:
that great Joe Williams' voice,

deep and rich, not like God's voice—
I wouldn't say that, would I? but a man's
voice, trained in the days of enunciation,
and strong, unfazed by all the baggage,
the weight of late nights, smoky places,

road; trusting the song, telling the story:
There will be many other nights like this...
and tears started to fall for all
the things I had loved and abandoned,
for too many deep cuts

and not enough standards,
the other you that I could never be,
and that was the moment the driver chose
to reach inside his denim jacket
and offer me his pint of Thunderbird.

Now I loved Thunderbird:
sweet, fruity bouquet, smooth finish,
and change back from your buck.
And if you happened to run out of gas
a pint would buy you fifteen miles.

But because I was so deep into the song,
I motioned him off till I had heard it out
all the way to *I may dream a million dreams
but how can they come true
if there will never ever be another you.*

The instant that the last chord died
I thought, "What have I done?"
But I couldn't ask him for a drink now,
I had to wait for him to offer. Why?
I don't know; I just knew that was

the rule that governed this particular test.
I had tried to keep my end of the bargain
with this new life, but Lord, it was hard.
My commitment flickered 51-49,
one way one minute, the other the next.

The Basie version has a bridge
catchy enough to be its own song,
where the singer sits down and the band
wanders off into a melody
totally different, but related,

like a face you know you've seen before--
*"maybe down in Mexico
or a picture upon somebody's shelf;"*
but what you're really recognizing
is the long-lost brother face,

the Other You that's glimpsed in mirrors,
out of the corner of your eye—
but that doesn't explain my love for it either,
so many jazz renditions have those bridges,
jazzers love to invent them...

I asked for help, as they had told me to—
premeditating I would tell them later,
"I did what you said; it didn't work."

Even as I asked, I had the reservation
if he offers that bottle again

all bets are off, and once I started,
I didn't kid myself that I could stop.
And wherever he dropped me,
I would hoof it toward
the lights of the nearest town

and drink till closing in whatever
roadhouse came out to meet me.
It seemed like my whole life
was a long string of these 51-49's,
never knowing whether to truck it

through another day indistinguishable
from every day before it
or distinguish this one with
the gesture that they couldn't take away
and say fuck it

and pick up the pieces later;
and every wrong decision brought down
all the rights that went before.
It was just *so hard,*
so *impossibly* hard.

Maybe that's what it was about that song.
I used the word "tension" before,
but that was a wrong word;
there wasn't a gram of tension in it,
the arrangement made it all seem so

easy, have it both ways.
Granted, there'll never be another you,
but there's another fox around the next bend
in the road, and I can live with that.
I can live with that.

The driver never made that second offer,
let me off at a hilltop intersection
where I scanned the horizon
and saw only darkness. Even in '62,
if you flew from Washington to Boston,

the whole east coast was a festoon of lights.
But it was my luck to be dropped off
at this one black spot that Megalopolis forgot.
Other adventures lay between Boston and me
that night, all funneling in one direction,

but they're part of yet another story.
This story we end more or less arbitrarily,
with young Jax standing with his thumb out
on a dark hilltop in Connecticut
on a mild Friday night in December,

curiously happy, supposing—
wrongly—that he'll be pretty high
before the moon gets very far across the sky,
asking for help in spite of himself,
singing like a defrocked choir boy,

I may dream a million dreams—
but never for one moment dreaming
the arrangements
that have just kicked in
in his life.

Footnotes to "For Joe Williams"

1. *The Justice Gulf Station*

Literally true. The road I was on was called the "Chief Justice [somebody] Highway."

**2. *And if you happened to run out of gas
a pint would buy you fifteen miles.***

Possibly true, but never actually tested.

**3. *like a face you know you've seen before—
"maybe down in Mexico
or a picture upon somebody's shelf;"
but what you're really recognizing
is the long-lost brother face,***

The quote is from Bob Dylan's "Lily, Rosemary, and the Jack of Hearts," which gets my vote as the greatest story-song ever written. I've always thought Dylan was hinting that Big Jim and the Jack of Hearts were long-lost brothers.

**4. *there's another fox around the next bend
in the road, and I can live with that.***

I once did this poem at a venue where poet Michael Brown was the MC. That night Michael shared the following anecdote.

> "After a show at Rick's Café Amercain [sic] in Chicago, Joe Williams liked to hold court in the big peacock chair in the corner farthest from the stage. One night I heard him say, 'Women are like public transportation. If you miss one, there will soon be another one coming along.' Later I found out Joe sang a song with that refrain."

Made me think I had a pretty good ear.

Christmas Story

Christmas Eve at 23,
I'd been sober 45 days,
which wasn't even my best yet.
Took the subway from the Ashmont meeting.
Remember meeting Joe W while I waited for the bus
in Broadway Tunnel that felt like a wind tunnel.
Joe was drunk, drooling, lost his teeth again,
looking like the Ghost of Christmas Past—
or maybe Christmas Yet to Come;
45 days, you just don't know.
I might have given him half a buck.

Finally comes the City Point bus,
driven by some poor schmuck
with noplace to go on the holiday,
resentful he's the only one here working,
but pleased to be getting double time;
the world is full of such conflictedness.
He didn't talk to me nor I to him.

The bus took me up Pill Hill
to Aggie Clayton's rooming house.
Aggie was in her 80s, mean and nosey,
but a lot of guys got sober in that house
without telling too much of their business,
and she had a soft spot for me,
used to serve me Red Rose tea
when I'd come in from meetings at 10:45.

"It's Canadian," she'd explain,
"and Canadian teas are better than American."
But Christmas Eve she didn't call me in,
and I was just as glad.

When I got back to the comparative warmth
of the room I shared with Owen G.,
it had been ransacked.

The little that there was to
go through had been gone through;
my laundry bag was dumped out on my bed.
We had nothing worth stealing,
and I didn't know what to make of it,
so I just started putting stuff away.

In a couple of minutes there was a knock on the door.
I opened and a stocky plainclothes cop
in the kind of big hat favored by Boston pols
put a hand on my chest and shoved me back into the room
and stayed right on me while a uniform followed him in.
He said, "You ever been in trouble before?"
I said, "I don't think I'm in trouble now."
He said, "Answer the question."
I thought for a second, sorting out
the things they could find out about,
and said, "I got in some trouble in the service."

Right answer.
He said, "Everybody got in trouble in the service."
He asked, "Where's your roommate?"

I said, "I don't know. He never came home last night."
"Where were you last night?"
"AA meeting/Christmas party at Gate of Heaven."
"How do you know Owen?"
"From AA."
"You know he's a career criminal?"
"Hey, a lot of guys in AA've been in prison."

About that time he wandered to the nightstand by my bed,
and picked up a copy of Shakespeare's "Julius Caesar."
I could tell it wasn't the first time that he'd seen it.
He said, "You read this shit?"
I said, "Yuh, it's not one of his best,
but a great play by any other standard."

It wasn't a lie, exactly. I had read the play in school,
and I was pretty sure I remembered the critics' judgment,

and if I hadn't, I didn't think this particular guy
was going to trip me up on that particular score.

But the fact was, I had never actually
opened up this particular paperback.
Owen had come in from the drugstore across the street
one Sunday afternoon a week or two before
and tossed it onto my bed.
"You read shit like this, don't you?"
I said, "Yuh, sometimes."
He said, "Well, I got it for you."
I said, "Thank you, that's really nice."

I somehow knew he hadn't paid for it.
I'd seen it on one of those revolving racks
in perfect position to be slipped into his
hip pocket while the druggist's back was turned,
and I'd have bet anything I had that I'd just become
a receiver of stolen merchandise.
But actually I was moved, although
I didn't let on; we never did.

But getting back to Christmas Eve,
I got the sense that the detective had decided
that whatever it was he was investigating,
the perpetrator did not read Shakespeare,
and from there it was like a baseball game where
one team scores fourteen runs in the first inning,
the rest was just playing out the string.

He told me apologetically he had to
take me down to the station house
and hold me till the morning shift came on
when they would interview me and let me go,
and that's what happened.
They served me coffee; I was treated well;
I had to ask to be put in a cell
so I could sleep.

They gave me a newspaper,
saying, "Read about your friend,"
and page two of the *Record* was a headline,
"COPS NAB OLD PRO GUNMAN,"

in which they called Owen "the most
dangerous man in Massachusetts."

This time they'd caught him
sticking up a liquor store in Brighton;
his young accomplice got away.
Owen got a fresh 15 for that.
I saw him in the paper again a few years later
when there was trouble at Walpole
and he was spokesman for the prisoners.

From personal experience I can say
that as long as he was clean and sober,
he was a good guy.
The world is full of such conflictedness.
And true that if it hadn't been for him
I wouldn't have slept that night in a cell—
not my first such night, by the way,
but my last—so far—
still, credit him providing me
not a Christmas card per se,
but one that said Get Out of Jail
Free on Christmas Day.

Wherever he is now, I hope somehow he knows
that there's at least one person here recalls
a gift he gave them still,

one who prays that when the angel cries,
"Peace on earth to men of good will!"
it might be recognized
there was a time when Owen
sort of qualified.

Footnotes to "Christmas Story"

1. Christmas Eve at 23,

Probably the only line in the poem that isn't literally true. The story actually started on Christmas night.

2. Remember meeting Joe W.

Joe W. was an interesting guy. He came to AA for eleven years, almost always drunk, looking to bum a quarter. The last time I saw him he had been sober for eleven years. He told me he was sober because some guy at a meeting had said to him, "Joe, they say there's no such thing as a hopeless alcoholic. But if there is, you're it." Joe told me he got sober just to prove that guy wrong.

3. in the kind of big hat favored by Boston pols

"Pols" are politicians. The word "politician" gets its full pronounciation in Boston with roughly the same frequency as the word "gasoline".

Cornerback

(Step Two: Came to believe that a power greater than ourselves could restore us to sanity)

Those first days I was like
a lonesome end
sleepwalking through my routes
knowing the ball would never come to me

and my disease was like
a cocky cornerback
checking me so hard
coming off the line

he took the wind out of me
backpedaling in front of me
as fast as I could run
his eyes glued to my beltbuckle

trashtalking all the while
"Who you shittin?
you think you can beat me?
I go backward faster

than you go frontward.
You think you got moves?
I can undo your shoes
while you puttin

your candyass moves on me.
Give it up and get it over with.
Why you wanna waste both our time
with your pathetic routes?"

He'd be in my face
every waking hour—almost.
And sometimes I'd wake up
tangled in twisted sheets

with his voice echoing in my head:
"Who you shittin?
You know what you are."
The only exception was

meetings; the moment I walked in
and heard the joyful buzz—
sanctuary, like being in the huddle,
surrounded by brothers.

But when the meeting was over,
and I'd walk out into the darkness alone,
he'd be back inside my shirt
all the way home:

"Hey, lush, there's a packy.
Hey, rumdum, there's a bar.
We can get good and drunk in two hours.
You know you can't keep this up forever.

Why you wanna put us through this?"
But he loved this shit;
this was what he lived for.
Four weeks, five weeks, six.

His taunting got to be like
elevator music—sure, not exactly
what any sane person would choose
to have running in the background,

but the operative word there is
background. Till—
it must have happened like this—
till one night I walked out of a meeting

and the cold air hit my face
and my eyes adjusted to the semi-dark
and I was wide open.
Maybe he was blitzing,

maybe he had picked up somebody
on a crossing route,
some poor bastard
still shaking off his last drunk

who left ahead of me
and cleared the zone.
But me?
I was running free,

and I've been
running free ever since.
And the funny part is at first
I didn't even notice he was gone.

Footnote to "Cornerback"

1. Hey, lush, there's a packy.
In Boston, liquor stores are often referred to as "package stores," or "packies."

Arthur M.

In the state of Washington, we celebrate AA anniversaries, or "birthdays," for a month at a time. At the beginning of every meeting, the chairperson asks if anyone is celebrating a birthday this month, and the people who have birthdays can be pretty sure they'll be called on during the meeting. The last Thursday of the month my particular group has an open meeting at which the coins are given out. I celebrated my 34th anniversary this month, and our birthday meeting was this morning. It turned out to be one of the most emotional meetings I've ever attended.

At this particular meeting we always start off by reading How It Works, the Traditions, and the Promises. Then somebody reads from the "Daily Reflections" and starts the discussion by talking about what they just read. Today I was that somebody, and the reading had to do with getting our own house in order so that we could do some good for someone else. It made me think of my early days in the program and Arthur M., and I told this story. (I'll probably tell it a lot better here because at the meeting, I kept choking up with tears and losing words.)

My early days of sobriety were tough, though no tougher than a lot of other people's. My health was broken for a while; I must have had the flu, or maybe walking pneumonia. My aunt would make me a potion of honey, lemon juice, and onion, in a little syrup bottle, and sometimes I'd take it out of my overcoat pocket at a meeting and take a big slug of it to stop my coughing, and people would think it was booze. Sometimes I'd fall asleep at the meeting, and they'd think I was passed out.

But I kept coming. Almost all the meetings were speaker meetings, and then as now, there were some great speakers around. People would say, "AA is not for those who need it, it's for those who want it." I needed AA to save my life, but what I *wanted*, what kept me coming, was the laughter and the stories, the entertainment value.

Arthur M. was one of those speakers you would come to meetings hoping to hear. If you saw him walk in and the group that had the commitment hadn't shown up yet, you'd say a little prayer that the group would get lost and there'd be a pickup meeting and Arthur would be asked to speak.

Whenever he'd speak, he'd start off talking about being a fish out of water, how he never felt at home in anything until World War II, the marines in the Pacific, the camaraderie and the killing, and how he cried the day the war ended because he knew he'd never feel alive like that again, like part of something, with a purpose. In civilian life he was a pharmacist, inherited a big drugstore. He told of all the years he kept himself going on terpin hydrate of codeine, GI gin, treating a post-nasal drip relentlessly for seven years.

He was a hero to me, one of those larger-than-life people who transform a room when they walk into it.

One Thursday night at Fields Corner, I was sitting toward the front (as I had been told to do), and Arthur sat down directly behind me with a friend of his. Arthur started talking out of the corner of his mouth the way he did, in that combat-captain voice of his; he said, "You know what I love about this program? I love watching these guys come in, you see them at their first few meetings, they're all beat up, hunched over, their eyes are always on their shoes like they were picking their way through a minefield. But they keep comin', and pretty soon they're standing up straight, smiling and laughing, looking you in the eye. And you get to see the life flowing back into them, one day at a time. *That's* what I love about this program."

And of course I'm hanging on every word, because I feel I'm privy to the real skinny, not merely what the hero Arthur M says from the podium, but what he confides to his friends, in private.

Then he said, "Now you take this young guy sitting in front of us..." And I felt my soul expand inside my chest, and a never-to-be-forgotten thrill went through my body as a little bit of that larger-than-life magic rubbed off on me. (And even today, almost fifty years later, as I proofread this passage for the umpteenth time, my heart skips that same beat and my soul clicks its heels yet again.)

That was 1963. Flash forward to the mid-nineties, a discussion meeting in Chelmsford, Massachusetts. A young guy walks in a little late and sits across the circle from me. Our eyes meet, and we recognize each other, and we nod and smile, the little nod and smile that signify, "Glad to see it's still working for you too." I remember him when he was a newcomer in Nashua in the eighties. I might have driven him to a few meetings.

Pretty soon it's his turn to talk, and he starts talking about how much I helped him in his early days, and I'm thinking, "This is always nice to hear, but this kid is making this shit up; I never did anything special for him."

And that's when I thought of Arthur M. And I knew that if he had been sitting across the circle from me today, and I had told that story about what he said to me—to my back, actually— and how much it meant to me, he would be sitting there thinking, "I never did anything special for this guy..."

And eventually I came to see it as a category, capitalizable: this is What Old-Timers Do. And it's one of the things I love about this program, this osmosis that takes place almost automatically, by bringing these hurting units, all their nerve ends out, into even the most casual contact with the serenity, the restored sanity, the awakened spirituality of the old-timers sitting beside them—or behind them, as the case may be.

That's the story I tried to tell, in a fumbling, stumbling way, at this morning's meeting. From that point it turned into a sort of gratitude meeting, and I swear, of the people who spoke, at least half cried, male and female. There was a young woman who was celebrating her first anniversary who started off talking about the family members she had invited who hadn't come. She said that when they realized they had forgotten, she hoped they would feel like shit. But a few minutes later she was talking about playing soccer with her daughter, and she was crying tears of gratitude. A man who is not an alcoholic, but who likes to come to the open meetings with his wife and son, asked if he could speak, and told us that to him, we were all heroes. He said, "I don't think I'm man enough to do what you people do. Sometimes I wish I were alcoholic so I could share what you have."

It went on like that. People made trips to the Kleenex box. I used up all the paper towels in all my pockets. When Carol got home and I tried to tell her about it, it started all over again. Why does telling that story affect me that way? It's not a particularly dramatic story. I think of what I once heard the poet Mark Doty say: "I don't know what my feelings are until I find the words for them." Today I found the words to tell that story, and I unlocked some feelings I never knew I had.

Footnote to "Arthur M."

1. Commitments

AA meetings are generally divided into two formats, speaker meetings or discussion meetings. At a speaker meeting one or more individuals will speak, usually telling their personal story, while everyone else listens; the speakers are most often pre-arranged. At a discussion meeting, everyone is eligible to speak. Many meetings work some combination of the two formats, most commonly with a single speaker followed by a general discussion.

When I was getting sober in Boston in the 60s, the vast majority of meetings were weekly 90-minute speaker meetings. The secretary of the South Shore group would approach the secretary of the Fields Corner group and propose an exchange of "commitments." Dates would be agreed upon, and on some subsequent Friday night, Fields Corner would send a delegation of four or five speakers to South Shore. On a subsequent Thursday, South Shore would return the favor.

Connoisseurs of meetings always liked to know in advance what group was putting a meeting on. If it were Marlboro, you had a chance of hearing John the Indian; South Boston, Jimmy Logan or Eddie McGann; Arlington, Andy Johnson; Providence, Red Head. (I can use last names because they're all dead.)

There was a guy we called Ticky Dicky who liked to get to meetings early and make friends with whatever group came in to put on the meeting. He would like them so much that he would join their group on the spot, regardless of where they were from (AA has no rules to prevent this, or to prevent much of anything else). He was often able to talk his way into a speaker's slot the same night. He'd begin his talk with the more or less formulaic, "My name is Dick and I'm an alcoholic and a member of this group and eleven other groups." Sometimes we'd get to hear Dick's story two nights in a row. The old-timers would shrug and say, "Whatever keeps him sober."

Waiting for a Dudley

In January of '63
it snowed every night.

I was getting sober.
I'd take the bus from South Station
to Aunt Kathy's in South Boston
for supper--usually a steak,
maybe tough and stringy,
but always tasty,
dripping in its own juices
and the butter it was pan-fried in.

After a short nap
I'd drag my grudging body
up off the couch
and out to a meeting.
Uncle Bill would say,
"Where you going tonight, Jax?
the holy jumpers again?"

At the corner of M and East 4th
there was a cleaner's
with a recessed doorway
where I'd wait
out of the weather
for a City Point bus
or a Dudley.

The doorway went in some ten feet,
tile floored, sloping slightly,
narrowing toward its inner, upper,
darker end.

There were holes in my loafers.
I could never make the doorway
without getting my feet wet.
And every night

at seven-thirty
it would be snowing.

Shaded bulbs on goosenecks
hung out over the sidewalk
shining down generous cones of light
bright enough to read by.

Deep in my doorway
I'd look out from dark
at big lazy snowflakes, numberless
floating and swirling in the generous cones
falling so slowly that it seemed
some of them were destined
never to reach the ground.

Without listening I would hear
the soft damping of all sound
that is itself a sound
and every snowflake
was a promise
of peace to come.

It has come slowly.
Peace does come slowly.

But every promise has been kept.

Footnote to "Waiting for a Dudley"

In South Boston there is an expression that can come up in any situation in which someone gets caught napping. For example, if you're playing baseball and you get picked off or you miss a sign, they'll ask you if you were "waiting for a Dudley." Dudley is the name of one of the MBTA bus routes that run through the community.

Frank & Dewey

Step 12: "Having had a spiritual awakening as the result of these steps, we tried to carry this message to alcoholics, and to practice these principles in all our affairs."

It used to be they'd point
a guy out to you and whisper,
all hushed and reverent,
"He does a lot of Twelfth Step work."

And in those days before detoxes
that meant going where they lived—
into the three-deckers and the
rooming houses, talking to drunks

over instant coffee at kitchen tables,
or where they sat on the side of the bed
in their undershirts, shaking,
never meeting our eyes.

It meant telling our stories
to an audience of one as though
both our lives depended on it—
because, you know, they did.

And in those days there were
giants in the earth, and the most respected
Twelfth Steppers in the Bottom of the Barrel Group
were Frank and Dewey.

Once, in the raucous moments just
before a meeting, I was talking with Frank
when Dewey came rushing in
out of the cold all excited

not even stopping to hang his topcoat,
picked his way to Frank across
the loud, laughing, smoking room.
Over the din he announced,

"Frank, I just came back from
a Twelfth Step call in an apartment
house up by Codman Square.
The guy who called me, drinks—

well of course he does,
he called me. His wife drinks too.
Their son drinks;
the daughter drinks.

Why wouldn't they,
with those two for parents?
The wife's brother lives with them,
and he drinks.

The people upstairs drink.
The people downstairs drink.
The manager of the building let me in,
and I smelled booze on him.

Everybody in this
whole apartment house drinks.
Frank, I've found us
a gold mine."

Footnote to "Frank & Dewey"

1. Bottom of the Barrel Group

There really was a Bottom of the Barrel Group. It met in Roxbury on Saturday night. I went to a meeting there the first night I was sober. But Frank and Dewey were members of the Fields Corner Group in Dorchester, which met on Thursday night. The incident described in the poem actually took place at the Fields Corner meeting. I exercised poetic license.

The Samaritan

I got into AA in the sixties; back before Boston
even knew it was a racist city, I joined a group
in Southie called the Good Samaritan Group.
I was the kid in the group and Frank F. was
the coffeemaker with lifetime tenure, one of the old-timers.
Sometimes on a Sunday night I'd get there early
and help him set up the hall—weekends were tough for me,
I was glad to see the end of them, and it was a safe place.

They say public speaking is the biggest fear
Americans have, but you'd never know it by AA;
I'm constantly amazed at the eloquence
and storytelling of everyday drunks.
But not Frank F.

Frank was a colorful guy, a longshoreman, but he was
one of those rare AAs who couldn't speak at meetings,
and the only way to hear his stories and his theories
was hang out with him as I did, and though I'd have denied it
at the time, I know today that what he was giving me
was love.

Frank's favorite theory was that alcoholism was a disease
of the soul, that the alcoholic was a seeker after something
unknown, who settled on alcohol because it seemed
to be the next best thing to that unknown, and that
the unknown thing that we all craved was in fact
God, and that was why the only remedy for the disease
was spiritual.

Somewhere along the line we got talking about black people,
me wondering why there were so few of them in AA,
him explaining to me, as we unfolded the chairs for the meeting,
that black people couldn't be alcoholics because alcoholism
was a disease of the soul and black people didn't have souls.

I felt bewildered, betrayed by somebody I trusted,
yeah, somebody I maybe loved. Prejudice,
bigotry, racism—undeniable, inescapable,
inexcusable. But I bit my tongue. After that
I continued to help him set up the hall, but I
stopped coming early enough for those long talks.
He didn't seem to notice anything had changed.

A few months later when Joe S. joined the group,
I wondered what would happen, because Joe was black.
I was very afraid there'd be fireworks,
and if I had to take sides, I knew that
Frank would feel I had betrayed him.

But in the weeks that followed, a strange thing happened.
Well, not so strange in some ways, I suppose.
In AA there's a sort of natural progression—
when I helped Frank set up the hall on Sunday night,
I was probably replacing somebody else who had
needed to do that job for awhile, but who had moved on;
so it wasn't strange for me to be replaced in turn.

What *was* strange was that my replacement
was Joe S. By the time I'd get to the hall,
Frank and Joe would have it all set up,
and they'd be deep in conversation
over the perking coffee. I'd hear Frank
telling Joe the same great stories he'd told me.
Sometimes Joe's laugh would boom out of the kitchen
and I'd wish I could be back there with them.

When it was time for Joe to get a sponsor,
he asked Frank, and when Joe got his medallion
for a year of sobriety, Frank faced his greatest fear
and got up in front of everyone to do the presentation.
When they hugged each other at the end of it, it looked
as if Joe was as proud of Frank as Frank was of Joe.

Now you probably think I'm going to make
some big point about conversion here,
but I don't think conversion is what happened.
I believe that Frank F. went to his grave
convinced that black people don't have souls,
that in that sense, he died a racist.
But when he looked at Joe,
he simply didn't see a black person.
I don't know if he ever discussed his theory with Joe,
but if he did, I'm guessing Joe just blew it away
with one of those Eddie Murphy laughs.

The only way I can explain the love Frank
gave to Joe goes something like this:
there are a lot of people who talk a good game
when the subject is brotherhood and tolerance,
but let the wrong person move next door
and their talk goes out the window,
all they can see is real estate values;
when confronted with an actual human being,
they don't walk their talk.

Maybe there's a symmetry;
maybe people who talk bigotry
are capable of the mirror-image inconsistency.
Frank F. talked a good game of racism,
but confronted with a human being in need of help,
his talk went right out the window
and all he could see was a brother.

I don't know.
This theory of mine is a curious one.
The heart is not in the right place.
It seems to have everything backwards.
But for some reason, I find hope in it.

HATCHECK

Step 3: "Made a decision to turn our will and our lives over to the care of God as we understood Him."

Every time we talk about this step
somebody says
I'm not very good at this.
I turn it over one minute
then I take it back the next.

As though God were some
disinterested
hatcheck girl,
preoccupied, gum-snapping,
never meeting our eyes.

I sit back and I listen
and I watch these people who say
they aren't very good at this.
Year by year,
week by week,

I watch them changing
till I look around and see
people I would trust
with my life
there, there and there

and I think,
As far as I can see,
these people
are doing almost everything right.
And sure, I see them at their best

when they come here.
And sure,
we all talk the talk
a little better than
we walk the walk—

but there is this too,
that we listen to our talk.
And it may be true that our talk
is always running a bit ahead,
but our walk is forever

catching up.
And if these are the people
who every time we come to this step
say, "I turn my will over,
I take it back,"

then I conclude
that must be the way
it's *supposed* to work.
Which makes sense only
if we allow the possibility

that the will we turn over
and the will we get back
are not quite exactly
the *same* will, that in those
few moments or maybe seconds

that it's been out of our hands
it has been subtly altered.
We produce our ticket
and the girl—
for whom we leave

a grandiose tip,
perceiving her now as
extraordinarily lovely—
the girl retrieves
for us our hat

and there could not be
another hat like that

on the Atlantic Rim,
and entirely familiar
in the way it sits our crown…

Only now,
without our knowledge, there's
another eentsy microchip
imbedded in the brim
to make it

just a tad simpler
for the hatcheck girl
to get to us
when we
need her.

Kenmore Square

Step 9: Made direct amends to such people wherever possible, except when to do so would injure them or others.

I knew a poet who would make
a couple hundred copies of a poem
and stick them in a pouch,
like a mailman
who wrote all the mail himself.

Saturday mornings
he would walk Commonwealth Avenue
from the Public Gardens
all the way to Kenmore Square
smile at everyone he met,
and offer each a poem.
Most people accepted them.

At Kenmore he would turn
and start back Commonwealth,
conscientious to retrace
the same side of that
gracious boulevard,
and he would reclaim his poems
from the sidewalks and the gutters
where they'd been discarded,
and he would stuff the pieces
back into his pouch.

We watch others go through life
leaving bodies strewn behind
and wonder vaguely
what our own trail looks like.
Bless those brave enough
actually to walk
that backward track.
They walk it for us all.

Footnote to "Kenmore Square"

Back in the 70s, I really did know such a poet. But I wrote the poem without making any connection to AA. It was some years later that an AA relative read it and said, "This is about the 9th Step, isn't it?"

To the Beautiful Young Mother Who Misunderstood Me at the AA Meeting
for Abigail

When I talked about passing on the gene,
I think you stopped listening maybe too soon.
Clearly, you did hear me when I said most
people come to AA *after* they've had their kids.
But for you and me who got the program young,
this was the 800-pound gorilla in the bedroom that
nobody ever acknowledged; we had to find our own
answers whether we were doing the right thing
having children when we knew that we were
probably perpetuating some alcoholic
snarl from our DNA.

Maybe I'm violating some unwritten convention just
mentioning it; if so, I apologize, but understand
that sooner or later *somebody's* going to ask
Does that gorilla belong to anybody here?
Maybe there should be one of those little
free pamphlets on it.

So is it right for alcoholics to breed? Judging on
the horrendous evidence of our own experience,
what we did to those around us, do we want to
watch our children go through that? You'd think
there would be prosperous, childless legions who
had answered that question No, but I haven't
met any of them, and what I went on to say was

Yes; Yes is the decision that we make, and Yes,
I think it is the right decision. Right for exactly
the reason you so eloquently stated:
the measure really is Would *I* be
better off if *I* had not been born?

There were surely times I thought
the answer to *that* was Yes, nights I went

to sleep praying I *would* die before I woke;
but those nights and times are so far now in the past
that all I feel for the poor bastard who endured them is
a sort of disinterested compassion, like looking at
photographs of shark-bite survivors.

And from where I sit today, the harder question
for me is, Would I have wanted to be born
and *not* be alcoholic? Because I can't imagine
what that would be like, what *I* would be like;
I don't think I would like me.

Still, as you and I both know, it's harder
still to watch it happen to someone you
love, especially when you think they
caught it from you—to see them drift into
the half-life, to listen to their half-truths turn
to outright lies, to feel again, through them,
humiliation of never being able to speak
truth to love—indeed, to come to wish
that no one *did* love us, so we might self-
destruct in peace, maybe not painless, but
anesthetized…

The decision that confronts us alcoholics
is the same one every couple has to make,
just a little more focused.

There are so many things to fear
that we could all be survivalists,
our windows sealed with duct tape,
sheds full of dried beans and ammunition,
and still we'd be vulnerable to some unanticipated
malady that got into the water…

The Iraqis, after all the hell they've been through,
still at their weddings fire assault weapons
at the sky to celebrate
something.

Every child we bring into the world
is just that kind of celebration,
not of the hope of invulnerability
or immunity or immortality, perfection—
no, every child is a celebration
of hope itself, an assault on heaven.

Snapshot at an AA Meeting

The bursting-with-pride
look on a little boy's face
when we applaud his mother
for eight days clean and sober.

Epithalamion:
A Few Words for Kathleen

We're here today to celebrate
the wedding of Kathleen and Mark.

Kathleen, when she was eight years old,
started coming with me to AA meetings on Friday nights.
That group had really good coffee, and as she would
make her way time after time to the coffeepot
I would lose sight of Kathleen, because she was short;
but I could follow her progress by watching the heads
turn to bless her with their eyes as she passed,
beautiful child that she was.

At the break they'd raffle off a Big Book,
and when the meeting broke up, Kathleen
would go from table to table collecting
all the discarded raffle tickets, which she would
bring home and store in a shoebox.
Why? I never figured it out.

Up came my anniversary, and my sponsor
was out of town, so I asked Kathleen
if she'd be willing to say a few words
in front of a roomful of grownups, and she was game—
Kathleen was always game. She had to stand
on a chair to reach the microphone, and if I remember
right, what she said was, "It is always an occasion
when someone celebrates their eleventh anniversary.
Jax?"

And if I'd been expecting something a little more—what?
personal? still, it was a great beginning for a ten-year run.
The next year she didn't need the chair,
and she wrote a poem that began,
"My dad is the best/he's been that way since birth/
It's a shame there's only one of him/on the planet earth."

Year three she brought Annie with her, and she said,
"Last year I read a poem for my dad's anniversary.
This year we're here to explain the poem."
Oh, would that every poet might acknowledge
that responsibility.

Kathleen's presence those Friday nights lit up
that big gymnasium, and a lot of people
who never got to watch their own kids grow up
came to look forward to her presentations
as a highlight of their year.
Tom G., who couldn't go with us
when we put on meetings in prisons
because he always set off the metal detectors
because he had a police bullet lodged
inoperably close to his spine,
said to me, "That kid is the best advertisement
for this program that anyone could ever see."

 And Billy T., a former three-hundred pound biker,
told me he had a daughter Kathleen's age—
"somewhere," and that every year he cried at
her presentation—but it was the *good* crying.

Now it's my turn to say a few words for Kathleen—
but she tied my hands a little,
made me promise not to make *her* cry.

So I'll address my comments to the groom.
Probably most fathers of the bride would admit
that they don't think there's a young man
in the world who's worthy of their little girl.

I want Mark to know that I don't feel that way—
particularly. But what I'm sure of is that Kathleen
and Mark have been extraordinarily lucky to find
each other. It's crazy out there; most of us feel fortunate
to find *anyone* willing to cast their lot with us, let alone
the *right* person. Today my heart is telling me
that this is right.

Now, Mark, about the dowry;
I'm afraid I have to ask to be dispensed from that
particular archaic tradition; it's not that I'm ungenerous,
just unemployed. But somewhere among Kathleen's
belongings, in a cellar or an attic
or at the bottom of a closet,
you might still find
a shoebox
full of raffle tickets
that didn't win anything.

If you find it, Mark, hang onto it. A lot of hopes
went into that box, the hopes of people whose
last names I never knew, people who didn't win
life's lotteries, didn't dodge all of life's bullets,
who once looked at Kathleen and took heart,
who loved her and left their tickets on the tables
in hope that they might be for her
tickets to a better life than they had had.

And any time you feel that life's
too hard, and you're too much alone,
take that box out and run your fingers
through those old raffle tickets, mix them up
real good, and think about how much luck it takes
to find the one person in the world
that we were meant to find.

Then go to the kitchen and put on a pot of some
really good coffee—and make enough
    for two.

Footnote to "Epithalamion"

Kathleen asked me to write a poem for her wedding, but one condition she imposed was that she had to see it before the wedding; she didn't want to cry and ruin her makeup for the pictures. So I sent her the poem with plenty of lead-time. I also recommended that she run it by Mark's family: they might not be happy to have it publicly announced that Mark was marrying into a family of alcoholics.

Kathleen and Mark liked the poem, and they gave a copy to Mark's mother. We didn't hear back and we didn't hear back, and we had begun to think that Mark's family—understandably—didn't like the poem for the event.

Then, at a bridal shower for Kathleen, the gift Kathleen got from Mark's mother was a coffee service for two.

NEPONSET CIRCLE
for my wife Carol,
the woman who drives me to Poetry

The Quincy AA Group liked to let Charlie drive
on their commitments. He was a careful driver
who stayed a mile or two under the speed limit,
and he liked to leave a little earlier than other people would.
But he never missed a turn or had to ask for directions,
and he always got the group to the meeting
on time.

Sometimes a newcomer would ask
why they had gone from Quincy to Brockton
by way of Neponset Circle—
there are back roads into Brockton, short cuts.
An old-timer would whisper, "*Shhhh.*
We know that there are quicker ways.
But Charlie likes to drive. And he can get us
anywhere in the world— as long as he starts from
Neponset Circle."

Most of us see the world as spider-web,
all sorts of intricate connections,
alternate routes. A good sense of direction
and a roadmap and we'll always find our way.
Charlie saw the world as a bicycle tire,
spokes crossing each other here and there,
but all of them running straight to and from
one heart.

Over the years a lot of newcomers got
too impatient to put up with Charlie's ways—
he wouldn't even take the Squantum Street cutoff,
they'd complain, and you could almost
see Neponset Circle from both ends.
Sometimes they'd maneuver themselves
into the front seat to make suggestions:
"*Charlie, this right goes straight to Hancock Street.*"

"*Yup, I know,*" he'd reply, and cruise right by,
while the old-timers puffed serenely in the back.
"*Insane,*" the dissidents called Charlie,
or "*anal,*" if they'd had Psych 101;
"*compulsive.*" As though we all weren't.
But he drove *them* crazy. Eventually
they'd take their own cars, thank you,
trust their own internal compasses.

And for a while, they would look good.
They'd leave a little later and be
sipping coffee smugly when Charlie's cadre
of newcomers and old-timers sauntered in.
But sooner or later they'd miss a turn and get lost
and a commitment would go by the boards, unmet,
and if it was a prison or a hospital,
there'd be no meeting there at all that night
and *that* was serious.

The old-timers knew that it would happen
because all the alternate routers had to go on
was their own sense of direction.
Charlie had Neponset Circle.
Carol, my love,
you're *my* Neponset Circle.

Footnotes to "Neponset Circle"

1. When I started doing this poem at readings, I'd introduce it saying. "This is a poem about a Boston traffic landmark and a guy my father knew in Alcoholics Anonymous." I said this mainly to protect my own anonymity. My father was in AA, but I have no reason to think that he knew Charlie. I heard about Charlie's driving habits my first year in AA. He was in one of the Quincy groups, but I don't remember his actual first name. "Charlie" just felt right.

2. from Quincy to Brockton
by way of Neponset Circle—

When I perform this poem, I indicate Quincy with my left hand, chest high, Brockton with my right hand, chest high, and then Neponset Circle with my right hand above my head. That's all the Boston area geography you need to know.

3. and if it was a prison or a hospital,
there'd be no meeting there at all that night
and that was serious.

If a group failed to arrive at a regular (non-institutional) meeting, they would just throw together a pick-up group of speakers from the audience. Institutions couldn't do that.

Substances

Sometimes when it's my turn I say,
My name is Jax, and I'm
constitutionally a stranger
to moderation in *any* of its forms.
That scene in Aliens

when the little squid-like thing
flies across the room
and fastens on someone's mouth
and it'll never come off
without killing the person—

we're like that, except with us
the squid didn't really fly
across the room, we **sucked** it.
That's how it was with alcohol,
and when I started drinking

I started sucking
cigarettes, and from the bottom
of my heart loved every drag that
ever scummed the cilia of my lungs
with the resin of its residue.

The only way I could stop drinking
was to hook myself on meetings,
they gave shape to the day, and it was
at those meetings I got onto
coffee, and by the way

when the last smokers in the USA
are bounty-hunted down, they'll
find them at AA meetings. Sometimes
watching reruns of Cheers I wonder
how Sam Malone stays sober,

you never see him going to meetings;
but then it's obvious,

he's upgraded *his* addiction onto women.
Well a little shape to the day
never hurt anybody. You go Sam.

When I started meeting coldness in
my first marriage I got into jogging,
like entering endorphin maintenance
to stave off heroine withdrawal; like
Mithridates, taking controlled doses of

known poisons; like lockjaw vaccination.
We are like birds, that in the winter
of pain migrate to Guatemala on the
wings of our substances; we are
incapable of residence, our essence

is long-distance flight, we dare
not risk the pain of owning anything;
even the paths of our migrations
are seasonal—and winter's never
more than nine months away.

I stopped drinking only when it
hurt too much to drink. I stopped
smoking when it interfered with
jogging. I stopped jogging
when the pain in my hips

started waking me up at night
for ice cream—which had to go when
my cholesterol reached escape velocity.
(I haven't had my cholesterol tested since—
but it's been fine.) Coffee

and Canada Mints and the aspirin
I take for my hips are eating at
the lining of my stomach as I speak.
All my life I've borrowed from Peter
against my body to pay Paul

for my emotions, and now Peter's
tracked me down and nailed
foreclosure to my door for
the fourteenth and final
mortgage on my organs

and all I can say is, *I gave
him a good run for his money.*
Soon the only thing left will be...
poetry. And maybe that's how it
was supposed to be: arcade of

substances that seem to ease
the pain, but all you're playing
is Whack-a-Mole, you bash it
here, it pops up there—
till suddenly you stumble on

the substance of your destiny
and understand at last
that all the pain
you ever gave the slip
was pain of not *doing* ***this***.

Footnote to "Substances"

1. That scene in Aliens

One of my publishers objected to the movie reference. He argued that people reading the poem in a hundred years wouldn't know what I was talking about. I told him that the possibility that people would be reading my poetry after *Aliens* had been forgotten wasn't high on my list of fears.

For Ruth Read,
on Her Seventy-Fifth Birthday

There's an old white house in Norwich—
    Church Street, to be exact—
That attracts the strangest people—
    not promote; just attract.

They come from all directions;
    they come in trucks and cars;
they come in creeds and colors;
    and all with wounds and scars.

I've come here many times myself—
    with family, with children, with laundry;
in horror, in terror, in love, and in pain,
    with furies hard upon me.

For this is the House of Healing,
    a haven for those out of hope;
alkies and junkies and put-it-in-front-of-me's—
    give me enough rope.

Here we find sanctuary,
    all strangers, come sister and brother.
The lady who lives here loves us;
    no less can we do for each other.

That's all, they say, that God wants from us;
    it's a lot like the way He works.
If you're looking for Him, stop here;
    you could look a lot further, and do a lot worse.

Footnotes to "For Ruth Read, on Her Seventy-Fifth Birthday"

When I talk about my "poetry career," I often describe the period between the late 70s and 1992 as a time when I had become disillusioned with poetry. I averaged maybe one poem a year, "and then only when the Muse held a gun to my head, threatening, 'If you don't write this one, I'll never give you another one.'" This poem is from that period, although in this instance, Ruth Read herself was the demanding Muse.

1. *Two notes about "alkies and junkies and put-it-in-front-of-me's—"*

a) Most people who write in English believe that when you have to pluralize a word that doesn't really have a legitimate plural form, you do it with an apostrophe: of numerics, for example, the 60's; of last names, the Kelly's. In this belief, most people are wrong: the correct forms would be "the 60s" and "the Kellys." In keeping with this principle, I should have written "put-it-in-front-of-mes," and in fact I did. But many people have had a hard time reading that, and consequently a hard time understanding the line. Forced to choose between grammatically-correct-but-unreadable and readable-but-wrong, I opted here for readability.

b) Within the Recovery community there are, on the one hand, those who think alcoholics are very different from drug addicts and, on the other, those who argue that addiction is addiction, whatever the substance. And in the middle probably a large majority who might lean toward one side or the other but don't think the question is worth fighting about. My personal addiction history is all about alcohol, although I've had enough surgeries to appreciate fully the attraction of pain-killers. But I have to admit that in my drinking years, I would have drunk, smoked, eaten, popped, injected, shoved up my ass, or otherwise ingested anything that anyone had put in front of me. It was just my good fortune that no one ever put anything else in front of me.

2. *"you could look a lot further, and do a lot worse."*

I was really proud of this line. Ruth's husband Frank had died a few years before this poem was written, and their love for each other was such that it would have been unconscionable to write this poem without including some mention of Frank. At the same time, how to deal with so sad a subject in a celebratory poem?

Of all the memorable things Frank had said, the one that I fastened on was something that Ruth told me he had said to her after first meeting my first wife: "Jack could have looked a lot further and done a lot worse." It was like sneaking Frank into the poem through a back door. I think he would have appreciated that.

Curiously, I had met Frank once several years before I ever met Ruth. Frank, who had risen to the rank of colonel and had been a base commander during and after World War II, had accepted a reduction to sergeant in the subsequent demobilization. When I started college, he was honcho of the ROTC program. We freshman were required to wear beanies, and anyone wearing a beanie was subject to being pressed into service by anyone who needed cheap (read "free") labor. It happened that a couple of my friends and I were hauled in to move some filing cabinets around Sergeant Read's office. He was gentle and soft-spoken with us, and appreciative; there was certainly nothing traumatic about the event, nothing at all remarkable. But seven-plus years later, when I met him as Ruth's husband, I remembered Sergeant Read.

Ruth Read Approaching 80

So many in my life today who weren't here
when I first met Ruth. Some depart,
others will come.
I acknowledge the pattern here.
More: the beauty of it,
the pacing. The stateliness.
The timing.

The memories this woman has.
Of Kansas City, Porta Rica, San Francisco,
Okinawa (in no particular order;
that's how they come out—no particular order).
Of the spiritual erosion of alcoholism.
Of a daughter who died too soon, too soon.
Of other daughters and a son,
none of whom has had it easy,
none of whom has ever asked for special treatment,
all of whom are still on their feet,
all of whom took enough hope from this family
to risk starting their own.
All the grandchildren, the great-grandchildren;
the adopted ones—myself and Marjorie, and April,
Michael and Ed and Debbie, Stephen and Amanda,
the brothers and sisters I've met,
the ones I've heard about, and maybe prayed for,
but haven't met;

probably sometime one I've met, but haven't heard about.
Maybe we crossed paths without knowing one another,
that we were of Ruth; perhaps only feeling for a moment
a wisp of something there, a glimpse of a flicker
of some intimate contact on some other plane...

Maybe there are even some I've neither met
nor prayed for nor even heard about.
"Though round the girdled earth they roam,
Her spell on them remains..."

There are institutions both sides of the Connecticut.
Who could keep track of us all?

Ruth could.
Those three address books describe
a web of relationship,
some of it blood, some marriage,
most of it by purest choice,
the choice, the decision, to love;
a web that crosses continents and generations,
drugs of preference,
religions—

we shall not hold it against her that she has a problem
with the idea that Catholics gravitate toward
short sermons and short Masses. I wish Amanda
hadn't let the cat out of the bag on that one;
I have been made to feel personally accountable—

religions and colors and sexual orientations,
maybe a barely detectable slant
toward good-looking young men—
I take that back.
All those addresses, all those birthdays.

Ah, the memories.
Of Frank, the stories we have heard,
the stories we will never hear,
were not meant to hear.
The love like a rock, like a mountain,
not consuming, not demanding;
there.
Those of us who saw that love
will always wonder about it:
was the world so different when they met
that an entirely different kind of bond was possible?
It is not possible today. The world has changed.
The chemistry between men and women has changed.

Before I met Ruth
I heard that someone had asked Frank,
"Why do you buy her the liquor?"
Frank had said, "Even if I knew that it would kill her,
and she asked me to get it,
I would get it. For her."

When I heard that story I thought,
"What a strange thing for a man to say."
I was wrong; it was what Frank *would* say.

The first time I went to a meeting with Ruth
it was in Woodstock, and she was royally drunk.
It was a discussion meeting, and she raised her hand to speak,
and she was called upon. She talked
about going out at dawn and watching a rose open.
I thought—as you may be thinking now—
"Oh spare me these poetic drunks."
I was wrong.
She had been out at dawn, and watched the rose.
She always had this thing for flowers.

There are yellow flowers by the porch in summer
and pink ones on the dining room table.
In the living room, more yellow ones,
but not like the first yellow ones.
She tells me what their names are,
but those must be the brain cells that I killed.
Many of these flowers are I-love-you presents;
the house is full of I-love-you presents.
She remembers where every present came from.
(Some are displayed more prominently than others.)

The kids she babysat for,
before the syllables in "daycare" had been joined.
My daughter Megan was one of them.
The day that her baby sister Caitlin died,
Megan was at Ruth's.
I went there straight from the hospital.

Ruth held me, then I held Megan.
Hold someone today.

In '72, after my one-night-stand,
I went to Ruth's to admit.
In '82, when I did something comparably destructive,
it was to Ruth's I went
to lick my wounds, begin to be forgiven.
How many of us have gone there?
to lick our wounds, to recover,
to begin to be forgiven,
to find a way to forgive ourselves?

Ruth is so proud of the kids she babysat for.
Her kids, she calls them, and keeps track of them.
And who can doubt she left her mark on them?
I know I must be wrong in this,
but I cannot but believe
that I could pick out from a crowd
by their civility, cooperativeness, and tolerance,
by something in the quality of their attentiveness,
the kids Ruth babysat for.
With maybe a six-percent margin of error.

When I brought her daughter Mary to the hospital,
Ruth lay there with all the tubes in her
and raved about how wonderful everyone was at the hospital.
When Ruth would pause for breath,
Mary would rave how wonderful
everyone at the airline had been.
She was sure her luggage
would arrive on the next plane.
(And she was right.)

And of course there is AA.
When I came back here in '64
you could almost count on your fingers
the people staying sober in the Upper Valley.
Tony and Romeo and Mike in White River,
Dotty and Win in Windsor,

Doc and Carlotta and Tommy in Woodstock, Bailey in Queechee,
Ned and Winnie and Frank and Pat to the north.
A few that I will have forgotten
but not many; not many.

Now there are so very many.
And who among us doesn't have at least one Ruth story?
She may not be the wisest person I have known,
but she can say very wise things.
I remember sitting with her in the living room
after my first marriage broke up and saying,
"My life is very exciting.
I'm going to lots of meetings now,
making a lot of new friends, getting hugs—
there are wonderful women in AA.
I like my life a lot. At the same time,
it feels like my life is over."

She said, "A chapter of your life is over.
The next chapter hasn't started yet."
And it was as if God had spoken to me.

When you tell her she has said something special,
she always says, "I don't know where that came from."

The implication, clearly, is that she does know.
She knows very well.

A kind word, when we're hurting;
or a stern one, when we slip into self pity—
she is not hesitant to volunteer to be the one
who decides when that line has been crossed.
Self-pity is the one thing, she often says,
that she cannot abide.

She is not a tough woman,
but she can get tough when love demands it.
You know you are in trouble
when she calls you by both names.
When the hands go to the hips,

the eyes flash—her eyes never get old—
when the little bantam body cocks itself;
"Well I swear, Jaxon Hardy, I never..."
Then we know it's time to repent, to pull up our socks,
to get on with things.
(Actually, last name *only* is even worse.)

It may be a fault;
she does not grieve enough,
she is sometimes impatient with the grief of others.
But if she is a little stern in this area,
she is sternest, undoubtedly, with herself.
Not necessarily wise, not entirely healthy,
but uncompromisingly consistent.

There are many people in AA who say they
wake up feeling grateful every morning;
Ruth is the only one that I believe.

She wakes up later now.
The clock is showing signs of running down.
For a long time, the energy level was the same,
the days were getting shorter.
Now you can detect some changes in the level of activity.
Sometimes there is pain; you cannot help but see it.
She would hide it if she could.

Ruth, it is all right.
We forgive you getting old.
We forgive you that your body has begun to resist
the demands you make on it in our behalf.
The time has come to rest upon your laurels.
The canvas is painted now.
There is no room for one more brushstroke.
Time to sit back
and gaze upon what you have made.

Footnotes to "Ruth Read Approaching 80"

1. About the time she turned seventy-nine, Ruth Read gave me notice that she wanted another poem for her eightieth birthday. My initial reaction, had it been spoken, would have involved the words, "How many poems...?" The task sat on my to-do list for months, but her birthday was still four months away when I sat down to take a shot at writing something for her. I was pretty happy with the first draft I came away with. Later that week, we got a call from Vermont that Ruth was dying. The family was gathering around her, and they wanted Carol and me to be there too.

"Ruth Read Approaching 80" has been edited slightly since I sat by her bedside and read it to her in the hospital three days before she died. She said it would make a good eulogy, so I read it at her memorial service three days after she died. I opted then to read it as I had read it to her, not putting her in the past tense. And that is how I've left it.

2. but not like the first yellow ones.

The poem was written about a month after I had taken part in a workshop led by Galway Kinnell. The benefits I got from that weekend were huge, but I didn't buy absolutely everything that Galway had to say. He read us one poem of his own that was rich with the names of things—plants, if I remember right. He said poets were responsible for knowing the names of things. I thought yes, but a little of that goes a long way; carried to extremes, it degenerates into obvious showing off. "But not like the first yellow ones" is my rejoinder to Galway's imperative. I've been waiting all these years to explain the joke.

In your face, Kinnell!

Ruth Read's Last Ninth Step

On a night in February, 1992 that wasn't the 14th, my wife Carol and I went out to dinner to celebrate Valentine's Day.

When we got home there was a message on the answering machine that Ruth Read was dying, and the family wanted us to come up to the house in Norwich, Vermont and watch with them.

I had known Ruth since 1964, when I went back to finish at Dartmouth, and when Ruth came into AA. I was sober then about two years, and I was riding in the car that brought her to her first AA meeting, on a Monday night in Woodstock.

I had gotten sober in Boston, where it was a simple matter to get to seven meetings a week on public transportation. But in 1962, AA hadn't yet much penetrated the stretch of Vermont-New Hampshire that they call the Upper Valley. Most nights of the week we had to drive 45 minutes to an hour to get to a meeting. There was one in White River Junction, but there were none in Hanover. And there weren't a lot of people staying sober.

But Ruth hit the ground running. After that Woodstock meeting, she never drank again. She and her husband Frank, the colonel, pretty much adopted me. My last semester at Dartmouth, I lived in their house. Their son Larry and I called each other brother; we still do.

Through the 70s and 80s I was back in Boston, working with computers and raising three remarkable daughters. We lived modestly; our one getaway every year was Labor Day weekend at Grandmother Read's—which is what she let my girls call her; they had no other grandmother.

On the Saturday and Sunday mornings of those weekends, I would go with Ruth to AA meetings, which by now were flourishing. And it seemed to me that about half the people I met at those meetings would tell me they had sobered up on Ruth Read's couch.

I was writing poetry off and on through those years, and in '87 Ruth asked me to write a poem for her 75th birthday, and I did. I mention that poem in this context because Ruth was going to turn 80 in 1992, and with plenty of lead-time, maybe over Labor Day in '91, she had asked me to write another poem for her 80th birthday. In all honesty, I have to admit to being a little miffed. At the time, I was writing maybe one poem a year, so as I looked at it, she was asking for a year's work. And was she going to want another one at 85? 90? Still, this was Ruth asking, and I said I'd give it a shot. But I didn't see how I could possibly live up to what I had written five years earlier.

The promised poem hung over my head like the dreaded term-paper that you put off till the last possible minute. Until I took a shot at it on a Sunday in early February. The weather must have been bad, or I'd have gone for a long run; and it must have been the Sunday before or after the Super Bowl. I sat down and started writing, and it was one of those blessed days writers have when everything flows. I'd been thinking about it for months, and gestation was complete. Unlike the earlier poem, this one was long, four and a half pages of very free verse.

I can't say it didn't need editing; I've never written anything that didn't need editing. But as a first draft, I was very happy with it.

So when we got the phone call inviting us to what I can only call the death-watch, I had the poem in hand.

Carol and I got to Norwich at night, too late to go to the hospital. We went straight to the old house on Church Street, right across from the Norwich Green. My "siblings" were all there: Larry, his twin sister Sarah (on whom I had had a huge crush when I was in college), and sisters Mary, from Chicago, and Barbara, from Texas, both of whom I felt I knew through Ruth's many stories; and who seemed to feel the same about me.

We sat around the living room that night, and I read them my poem. My tears flowed as I was reading it; I thought they would love it. But at the end, there was a long silence. Finally, one of them said, "Well! That certainly wasn't the woman that we grew up with."

And it occurred to me, for the first time, that almost all of them had been well out of the house, and mostly pretty far away, by the time Ruth got sober. The woman I had known was very probably a very different woman from the one that had raised them.

They began to talk, and an awful lot of pain was vented that night. Carol and I listened, dumb, respectful, maybe a little bewildered. I don't remember that we heard horror stories; objectively, I have to say that I didn't hear one story that was worse than some of my own childhood stories, and on balance I consider my own parents pretty wonderful.

But by acclamation the verdict of the room was that they had been brought up with abuse and neglect. And the great love that I had witnessed between Frank and Ruth had been a love that excluded everyone else—even their children.

Still, they had no hesitation about my reading the poem to Ruth the next day, assuming she was up to listening to it, and I did that, at the hospital, standing at her bedside, the pages of the poem in my right hand, my left hand in her hand, no hand free to wipe my eyes or my nose when my tears started flowing, as they did at unexpected junctures; that's always the way.

I try to write things honestly, always. In my body of work it's hard to find an unmixed blessing or an unmitigated tragedy. There was one passage in this poem where I came close to criticizing Ruth, because she really didn't have much patience with self-pity, and she felt that she had a very acute sense of when enough was enough. As I approached the reading of that passage I was nervous; it's AA policy that we don't take other people's inventories, and even if we did, we probably wouldn't do it at their deathbed. I needn't have worried;

when I read those lines she looked up at me with sharp nod and a fierce grin, and squeezed my hand with surprising strength. She didn't think it was a flaw at all.

When I finished the poem, she immediately said, "I want that for my eulogy." Then she asked me to sing Tequila Sheila, her favorite song of my singing, and she commanded the nurse into the room to hear it. Then she was tired, and I left and went back to the house where we all talked and waited; she wasn't expected to make it through the night.

My own parents had died suddenly, six months apart, when I was seventeen, so I'd never been in a situation like this, and I had then and have now no idea what's normal, or whether there can be a normal. Maybe normal goes out the window when a deathwatch is initiated with a eulogy. All I can testify to is this particular experience, and it seemed as if every human interaction less perfunctory than "Please pass the salt" was weighted with all the baggage of a lifetime. I'm not saying that we didn't laugh, because we did; we told stories that were genuinely funny, and stories that had never seemed funny before but that now made us laugh for reasons far removed from the comedic.

Maybe I idealize it now, from this distance of years; I'm sure I do. I remember all of us talking with absolute honesty; either we just blurted truth, or, if trying to say something complex, we tested our words before speaking them, tested them against rigorous standards of honesty and accuracy to which we did not routinely hold ourselves, honest people though we all routinely were.

Ruth didn't die that night, nor the next, and her extended family fell into an almost comfortable routine: what would we eat and who would shop; whose turn it was to visit the hospital and who would drive. We weren't digging in for the long haul, but we had no idea how long this might go on.

On one of those days, when it was the turn of others to visit the hospital, I actually got a chance to go out cross-country skiing on the snow-covered ice of the Connecticut River. I said a rosary for Ruth and my praying fell quite naturally into the rhythm of my skiing.

When I finished the rosary, I launched into Tequila Sheila, at full volume.

Over those days, there were also moments when one of my adopted siblings would catch me alone and share with me other stories about growing up under what can most charitably be called hard love. All these stories tended to be about something sad that happened to another sibling, something the speaker had been powerless to prevent or to assuage. No one was feeling sorry—directly—for themself.

On the third day, when it was my turn to be alone with Ruth, I offered to sing Tequila Sheila, but she said, "No, I'm in enough pain already." When I got settled she grasped my hand and looked at me fiercely and asked, "Why am I not dying? I'm ready to go. Why won't God take me? Is there something I've left undone?"

Among the twelve suggested steps of the AA program, there are two that I used to call "the forgotten steps," steps eight and nine, where we make a list of "all persons we have harmed," and make amends to them wherever possible. The prescribed process is carefully laid out in AA literature, consisting of an apology acknowledging the harm followed by some action aimed at restitution or atonement.

Because so many of us have said we're sorry and promised to do better dozens if not hundreds of times in the past, only to collapse even deeper into the depravity of our disease, many recovering alcoholics see the apology as the easy part and the atonement as the hard part. We postpone the apology in lieu of a time when we'll have earned, by our actions, some renewed credibility. And sometimes we come to feel that our actions have spoken for us; by the time we revisit the issue, it seems that the appropriate moment for the apology has long since passed.

The question that Ruth asked me that day was one that Carol and I had whispered about in the privacy of our little borrowed bedroom. The only possible answer we could come up with was that Ruth needed to say the words to her children. But when we considered the possibility of broaching the subject with Ruth, the prospect was forbidding. Far easier to volunteer Tequila Sheila.

Yet here Ruth was, asking—nay, demanding—that I answer that precise question.

I screwed my courage to the sticking place and said, "Have you ever told your kids that you love them, that you're sorry for the ways you let them down, and that you're proud of what they've done with their lives?"

She drew back her head and glared at me and said quickly, "They know that!"

I said, "Ruth, I think they need to hear it from you."

She pulled back even further and I braced myself for one last flash of her famous righteous anger, but instead she said, "Send them in."

And we did that. One by one they went into the hospital room, and one by one, after a few minutes, they came out, each one in tears.

That evening, while her extended family squeezed in over dinner around the dining room table across the river in Norwich, Ruth Read breathed her last. Or, as we say in AA, made the program.

The Divorced Catholics of Jaffrey, New Hampshire

A woman raised her hand,
in the vertical locked straight-arm
of kids who know they have the answer
and burn with a single-minded determination—

not enough that I know this,
I have to be the one who gets to say it.
My friend, a priest from the Paulist Center
in Boston, was talking in Jaffrey, New Hampshire,

about support groups for divorced Catholics—
"divorced Catholics" being a phrase
that by this time no longer had about it
the ring of *absolute* hopelessness.

In the instant that he opened for questions,
her hand went up with the eager abruptness
that sets off warning bells in anyone
who's ever tried to run a meeting of any kind.

She announced that she saw no point
in support groups; she argued that all Catholics
ever needed was daily Mass and communion,
a rich prayer life, and the occasional novena.

My friend was a gentle man, and he
moved on to take another question
with the gentle manner of one
inviting alternative opinions.

Moments later her hand was up again,
and we thought something said in the interim
had caught her interest. She was bright
and articulate, and at this point we still

wanted to hear what she had to say,
but she just reiterated that all we Catholics
ever needed was daily Mass and communion,
prayer, novena—like, "It's just you and me,

God. No need getting anybody else involved."
My friend observed that
in the experience of some of us, a little
human contact might facilitate the healing.

Moments later her hand was up again,
and Father Paul looked over the crowd
hoping for another hand, looked at last to me.
But I was staring fascinated at the woman.

She was attractive, late thirties maybe,
stylish (for Jaffrey, New Hampshire);
but no mystery why she'd been dumped.
I didn't have the balls to get in her way—

Or maybe I did, but I wanted to keep them.
He called on her again, with resignation this time,
and she recited her litany: Mass, communion,
rosary, God, novena, yada, yada, yada,

world without end amen. And I knew
what I wanted my friend to say to her,
I knew what I would say had I had the nerve
to raise my hand: that yes, she was right,

Jesus *had* said, "Ask, and it will be given,
knock, and it will be opened to you."
Beat on God's door, demand, Get me through this,
Father, I have done my part and you owe me.

God has no choice but to help us.
But I also knew with absolute certainty
that God would *rather* that we turn
each to the other in our pain,

would rather that our pain become a vehicle
for bringing us *together* than that it drive us
solitary to our incense-scented cells.
But if I said this the woman would ask,

"How do *you* know? Where does it say
in Scripture?" and I didn't know how I knew it.
I rummaged through my little store
of half-remembered Gospel stories,

but the loaves and fishes in
my memory resisted multiplication.
The session petered out like a poem
that's given up trying to be good

and settles for being over. I'd be
surprised if the divorced Catholics
of Jaffrey, New Hampshire ever got
their support group off the ground.

My friend didn't say to me on our way out,
"You should have rescued me,"
nor I, "You should have had an answer."
On the long ride home alone I kept thinking,

"Why am I so certain that I'm right?
where's my evidence?" I couldn't think of
one line of scripture that supported my case.
But there's a lot of time for thinking

on New Hampshire roads,
roads that took me past a lot of places
where I'd gone to AA meetings.
Till finally I made the connection:

I know because that's how AA works:
*our pain is the dynamic
compelling us together,*
and that's how God *wants* things to work.

I couldn't remember ever hearing anyone
say this, and I wondered if this was maybe
lost knowledge. Perhaps it was at the bottom
of the stone tablet that got broken,

that Moses had to reconstruct
from memory, and he, like most of us,
was less than perfect.
Or maybe it was *new* knowledge,

maybe this was something even God
didn't know he wanted until 1935,
when Bill W in desperation saw
the mc-squared part of the equation,

the part of "I have to talk to another drunk"
that says, "*because I need him
as much as he needs me.*"
I just wish I had seen this in time

to share it with the divorced Catholics
of Jaffrey, New Hampshire.
There might have been *somebody* there
who would have heard it.

The Sacrament

The guy next to me told me that this was his first time at this meeting. I asked him if he'd been to any other meetings and he said, "Two." I told him that part of the format is we ask if anyone here is at their first, second, or third meeting. "Just raise your hand and say your name and you're an alcoholic, and they'll pass a meeting list around with your name on it, and all the men will write their phone numbers on the back."

I know now that the practice is not uncommon, but in my many twenty-four hours, ours was the first such group I had run into. The first time I saw it happen I thought, "What a great idea." When I first arrived at AA, they told me to get a little notebook and collect a lot of phone numbers; but they left it up to me to do it. I got a few numbers, but I found it very difficult asking people. It felt like asking a guy out for a date.

I once knew a woman who had written a book about her recovery. She had a publisher for it, and they were trying to figure out what to put on the cover. They had decided on the woman, in silhouette, sitting in an armchair with a bottle of booze on the table beside her. But they also wanted some kind of a symbol of hope. She asked me for ideas. "What about a cross?" she asked.

I said that although AA's background traces to Christianity, the founders went out of their way to avoid any direct association with specific religions. The emphasis has been always on spirituality as distinct from religion. I couldn't come up with anything, so we took the problem to an old-timer. He thought about it for a minute and said, "A telephone."

I immediately saw the rightness of that. How many of us have begun our journey in sobriety with a phone call? Sometimes we made the call, sometimes somebody made it for us. I wonder if AA could have existed prior to the telephone.

For years I belonged to a group that ran an ad in the local paper every Friday that said, "If you can drink, that's your business. If you can't, we're willing to make it ours." Just that and a phone number. The number of people who got sober through that ad had to be in the hundreds.

At today's meeting, several people talked about the meeting list that was making its way around the room, picking up phone numbers. One guy said, "You can call me from ten in the morning to midnight. After that call Dan," and we all laughed at Dan's expense. A woman complained that she had written her number on hundreds of those lists, but not one woman had ever actually called her. A couple had stories about how those phone numbers had maybe saved their lives when they were newcomers, stories about dialing eight or nine or ten numbers before somebody actually picked up.

And I thought about the Saturday night in Akron, Ohio in 1935, when our fellowship was born, when Bill Wilson stood in a hotel lobby feeding nickels into a payphone until he found another drunk—"because I need him as much as he needs me."

Early in my sobriety a national magazine published an article trashing AA. The author thought we were too religious, that coffee was our new sacrament. Every five or ten years we see an article like this. Somebody thinks they have a better idea. They get a lot of publicity for awhile, but for some reason they always drop off the radar screen pretty fast.

I remembered that article today. I thought that maybe AA should have a sacrament. But it wouldn't be the coffee. It would be the meeting list that was going around the room collecting phone numbers—like the list Bill Wilson worked from in 1935.

When *he* was a newcomer.

Drunks: The Story of the Poem

For years in AA, I was haunted by the thought of all the alcoholics who lived and died before there was an AA to come to—the absolute hopelessness of their condition. Whenever I would speak at meetings, I'd want to talk about it, but I never did, because I was afraid I'd break down into uncontrollable weeping.

When I got serious about writing poetry (1992), one of my first inspirations was that poetry might be a way to say some of the things I had been wanting to say for a long time. In the writing of this poem, a strange thing happened. I sat down to write about all the people who died before there was an AA to come to, but almost all of the examples are my contemporaries, people I knew or knew of who died before they got the program. The guy who died of pneumonia in a furnished room was a man named Dennis M. who bought me breakfast the first Sunday morning of my sobriety. The one who died under the Southeast Expressway with a bullet in the back of his head was an ex-boxer named Tony V. whose brother was in the fourth grade with me. I didn't know the man who took his family with him; he was from the Westwood (MA) Group and he had a slip—it may have been his first night back to drinking. Ernest Hemingway, Dylan Thomas, and John Berryman also find their way in.

I have often read this poem at meetings, and when I do, I usually bring copies, because people always ask for them. When I first got on the Internet in 2000, the poem was there ahead of me on a number of Recovery websites. I've since found it on websites as far away as Saudi Arabia, Jerusalem, and Australia. It's very gratifying that so many people want to publish it. Of course I've never made a nickel from it. (Never made a nickel, true, but in October of 2007, on the strength of this one poem—and some long-term sobriety—they flew me in to Spain to speak at the Costa Brava AA Convention.)

Feel free to read the poem to any audience any time.

Author's Afterword

When I was 17, I had the world by the tail. I was an honors senior on scholarship at one of the great prep schools in the country, and I could write my own ticket to college. I was the oldest of four kids in a family that wasn't the Cleavers, but it wasn't bad by any standard. My father had gotten sober in AA in the early 1940s, and we had moved from three-deckers in South Boston and Dorchester to a two-story house of our own on the South Shore, with three acres of land and a barn that we didn't really know what to do with.

In September of my senior year my mother was killed in a car accident, and in March my father died of a heart attack, and everything fell apart. Within weeks of my father's death I had my first taste of hard liquor, a pint bottle of Bacardi Rum. That first pint lasted me a week. I'd take a sip before sitting down to watch TV, before starting my homework, before going out on a date. Suddenly the whole world was technicolor, everything was interesting; I had been half asleep and three-quarters bored my whole life, and now, for the first time, I was fully awake.

That was the first pint. When it was gone I managed to get another one. The second one lasted maybe 45 minutes. I got very drunk and very sick and I established the pattern of all my subsequent drinking experiences: I would drink as much as I could hold of as much as I could get my hands on as often as I could get my hands on it. My biggest problem was getting my hands on it, because at seventeen I looked about fourteen.

On the day of my father's funeral they came down from Exeter to tell me I was getting a full scholarship to Dartmouth. By the time I got there in September, I was a full-fledged and fully enthusiastic alcoholic. From there it went the only direction it could possibly go, downhill, and rapidly. I wasn't evil and I wasn't really dangerous—although it was just luck that I never hurt anyone while I was driving drunk, fighting to stay awake, or holding one hand over one eye. When I was sober, I could be charming and funny. But all I ever thought about was my next drink.

From a simple recitation of the sequence of events, it might sound as though I'm implying that I became an alcoholic because of the family tragedy. That's tempting, but far too easy. Looking back to earlier years, it's easy for me to see the personality seeds that sprouted under the irrigation of alcohol. I think my father was able to see them too; he was always trying to get me to read AA literature.

At the same time, I'm not one of the people who believe that alcoholism is caused by character defects. I've known hundreds of people whose defects look a lot like my own, and only a minority of those people are alcoholic. What is undeniable is that when my defects met my alcoholism, it was a match made in heaven.

So no, I don't blame my alcoholism on the death of my parents; it was going to happen anyway, and I've always been glad they weren't around to see it.

My drinking lasted just over five years. The only period of consistent happiness I remember from those years was the six weeks I was locked up in an Air Force stockade outside of Denver. They worked us pretty hard during the day, but they gave us three good meals and a warm bed at night. I couldn't believe how good I felt, or how happy I was. I remember singing at the top of my lungs in the shower one night, and the desk sergeant stuck his head in and yelled, "Hey! Perry Como! Knock it off! I'm trying to make a phone call out here." I thought, "This is a great life. This life would be perfect if I could only get a drink."

But eventually they discharged me and I was able to get a drink, and the disease took over again. Sometimes I put up a really obnoxious front—my first actual arrest was for "drunk and obnoxious;" I've never figured out whether that was a standard charge or one that they had invented for my behavior that particular night.

Certainly no great criminal, dangerous only by accident; but I truly thought I might have been God's biggest disappointment ever. He had given me so much to work with, and I was such a total fuckup. People would ask me if I thought alcohol might be my problem and

I'd say, "If only it could be that simple." But it turned out that it was that simple.

I came to my first AA meeting on May 20th, 1962. I knew that night that I was home. I wish I could say that I hadn't had a drink since, but this year (2012) I celebrated forty years of continuous sobriety. (Yes, that includes weekends, and yes, I do mean forty years in a row.)

My publisher asked me to write this section as an Introduction. I made several starts at that, and finally decided that I could do a better job on an Afterword. If this were an Introduction, I would have to try to convey to you in prose my love for AA, my gratitude for the fact that it first saved my life, and for the way it then informed every aspect of the life that it had saved.

I might talk about coming into AA at 22, when the average age was probably over 50, listening to heart-breaking stories from men who never got to watch their kids grow up, and knowing that I would get a chance to do those things right. Did I do all those things right? Of course not. Just enough of them to make all the difference in the world.

In an Afterword, I don't have to convince you of any of that. If you're reading this, I can assume that you've read what goes before, and if my love for AA hasn't already come through, there's nothing I can say at this point anyway.

WHY THIS BOOK?

I consider this book my legacy. Two of the great loves of my life have been poetry and Alcoholics Anonymous. Without AA, there wouldn't be any poetry in my life.

In the twelfth step of the AA program, it is suggested that we "carry the message" to other alcoholics. Maybe a book like this can convey that message of hope in ways that haven't been tried before, and reach people who might not be receptive to other means. Maybe it can generate hope in hearts where hope has been a stranger for a long time. Maybe it can enrich the sobriety of some who have already achieved it and who need an occasional dose of what art offers, the abiding sense that we are not alone.

WHY NOW?

It's now or never. I'm dying. No, I'm not writing this from my deathbed. I'm sitting up at my desk, fully dressed. As I write I'm looking forward to going out this Thursday evening to do a reading at a little coffee house that has been good to me in the past. I'll have to read sitting down, using supplemental oxygen, but my voice is still good and I'll probably hang around long enough to sign a few books afterward.

But I'm very probably going to die before you do. After almost two years of surgeries, chemotherapy, and radiation, a couple of weeks ago my wife and I decided against any further tests and procedures, and availed ourselves of hospice services. I'm very fortunate not to be in any particular pain, and I'm OK with the rest of it. There was a time I didn't expect to live to see 25; now I'm 73. The difference is, as Raymond Carver said, "all gravy."

Sometimes you'll hear an AA say, "I have a disease that seems to believe that it can kill me, and go on without me." I like to think that whatever little slice of the AA message I carry might somehow be able to go on without me.

APOLOGIA

Now comes the apology I owe you for the partial bait-and-switch in the title. The title suggests that this book is a volume of poetry, but a few seconds of browsing probably showed you that it also includes considerable prose. I could point to my poetic license, and make my stand on the ground that I have always been in favor of blurring all the dividing lines; that I believe that of all the categorical words defining literature, the word "poetry" is the only one big enough to include everything.

But there is also a less militant explanation.

This book was conceived as a slim volume of honest-to-God poetry. It's now a couple of years since I circulated the first cut to a dozen or so friends and colleagues to get their opinions on what to keep, what leave out. Some of these first readers were poets, some were in recovery, and some were double winners.

Most of the pieces in that first cut were conceived as poems before word one had been written. But in putting together that first cut, I also drew on material from a folder that I called "Meeting Notes." Sometimes an AA meeting will set off a chain of connections in my head that I find very exciting. On those occasions I sometimes write it all down when I get home.

A few of the poems in the first cut were the result of reworking prose from Meeting Notes. And as I browsed through Meeting Notes looking for other candidates I found some passages that could probably qualify under the general category of "prose poems."

And there were other pieces that no one could possibly mistake for prose poems, but I just liked them too much to cut them. What the hell? My pre-readers could make that judgment for me. As it happened, some of my pre-readers liked some of the prose better than some of the poetry. So I went with it.

The line got further blurred when from pre-readers and eventually from editors, I got questions about some of the references in the poems. In "Drunks," for example, what is the "Big Bed?" What are the Dropkick Murphys doing in there? I could have edited the poems to clarify, but that poem had stood that way for twenty years. It was true to the time and place of its writing, and I didn't want to compromise that. Footnotes seemed to be the solution that let me have it both ways. Not ideal, but I'm not the first poet to employ them.

And if I don't answer these questions now, who ever will?

Most important, when we considered alternative titles, was that without those five letters (P-O-E-M-S), there would be no indication on the outside of the book that there was any poetry involved at all.

ONE LAST EXPLICATION, AND A SMALL REQUEST

AA has two anonymity traditions which I consider sacrosanct. The result is that if this book is released in my lifetime, I can't put my real name on it. But once I'm dead, anonymity is moot. So if the name on the cover of the book in your hand is other than "John X.," you'll know that I've gone on to the Next Great Adventure. If you're a praying person, please say a little prayer for my widow. She made me very, very happy.

Acknowledgements

I want to acknowledge everyone who ever stuck out their hand to me at a poetry reading or an AA meeting; recovery is contagious. If no one were listening, no one would speak, and each of us would go to our grave keeping the secret that might have saved someone else's life.

But for this particular volume, special thanks to the hard-nosed cadre who stayed with me from the first scatter-shot everyone's-invited open camp to the barely recognizable distillation of what I hope were our best insights, intuitions, and wild-ass guesses at what some hypothetical God of our dubious understanding might be trying to tell us. Thank you,

Wess Mongo Jolley
Jodie K
Bill Mac
Carol McCarthy
Ryk McIntyre
Mary Pinkoski
Jon Sands
David R. Surette

And special thanks to Derrick Brown and Lea C. Deschenes. Special circumstances around the publishing of this particular volume have compelled me to ask for special treatment in a number of areas, and they have met me far more than halfway on every occasion.

Jack McCarthy

If You Like Jack McCarthy, Jack McCarthy Likes...

Scandalabra
Derrick C. Brown

The Constant Velocity of Trains
Lea C. Deschenes

Heavy Lead Birdsong
Ryler Dustin

Ceremony for the Choking Ghost
Karen Finneyfrock

Bring Down the Chandeliers
Tara Hardy

City of Insomnia
Victor D. Infante

In Search of Midnight
Mike McGee

1,000 Black Umbrellas
Daniel McGinn

Rise of the Trust Fall
Mindy Nettifeee

The New Clean
John Sands

News Clips and Ego Trips
G. Murray Thomas

Write Bloody Publishing distributes and promotes great books of fiction, poetry and art every year. We are an independent press dedicated to quality literature and book design, with an office in Austin, TX.

Our employees are authors and artists so we call ourselves a family. Our design team comes from all over America: modern painters, photographers and rock album designers create book covers we're proud to be judged by.

We publish and promote 8-12 tour-savvy authors per year. We are grass-roots, D.I.Y., bootstrap believers. Pull up a good book and join the family. Support independent authors, artists and presses.

**Want to know more about Write Bloody books, authors and events?
Join our maling list at**

www.writebloody.com

www.ingramcontent.com/pod-product-compliance
Lightning Source LLC
Chambersburg PA
CBHW060458080526
44584CB00015B/1466